Successful Motherhood

Successful Motherhood

DHYAN BABY
(A Language for Fetus)

Sri Kalyani; Murugan Santhanam

PARTRIDGE
A Penguin Random House Company

To order additional copies of this book, contact
Partridge India
000 800 10062 62
orders.india@partridgepublishing.com

www.partridgepublishing.com/india

CONTENTS

1   Motherhood..15

2   Foundation for human life 19

3   Spirituality & science in motherhood................. 22

4   It is a boon to have a baby 25

5   Child's expectation as a foetus........................... 28

6   A prenatal education and therapy..................... 32

7   About neurons and lord krishna's illustration 35

8   Conceptual period 40

9   Parent's mood and its impact on the child.......... 44

10   Mystery of our body.. 48

11   Genes, genes, genes! 50

12   About our brain and consciousness 54

13   Formation of sensory organs and how to train them? 57

14   Will the fetus learn? 63

15   Intelligence development..................................... 68

16   Month based pregnant therapies 80

17   Meanings of month based Pregnant Therapies ... 82

18   First Year Period... 104

19   Short stories 111

19-1 Moral code..112

19-2 To strike the balance 116

19-3 Desire or satisfaction-which is ruling us?........... 119

19-4 Proactiveness... 122

19-5 Dream, dream, dream..125

19-6 Gestation period - the natural law..................... 129

19-7 Real success of the society 132

19-8   Managing relationships 135

19-9   Learning a lesson from the tree 139

19-10   What is the real need to our children? 142

19-11   Mind washing!! 146

19-12   Spiritual enlightenment 150

19-13   Living spontaneously 153

19-14   What you think is what you are! 157

19-15   What is god's language? 161

19-16   5 'S' to our mind 164

19-17   Where the mind is without fear 167

19-18   Sharing the happiness to attain eternal bliss 170

19-19   Tunnel vision (to learn from the birds) 173

19-20   Learning to vent emotions 177

19-21   Mystery of mind! 181

19-22   Gratitude- the animal style 185

19-23   Let the fruit to ripe naturally 188

19-24   Neighbours' envy 191

19-25   No short cut for the success 194

19-26   Wasting food? you are fined! 198

19-27   Who stole my juice? 202

Dedicated to all expectant mothers all over the world who aspire for having gifted child who, in turn Change the future civilization.

ACKNOLEDGEMENT

ANUGRAHA

(Capuchin Institute for Counselling, Psychotherapy and Research) [Recognized by the Canadian Association of Pastoral Practice and Education & Affiliated to Madurai Institute of Social Sciences]

Sundar Wilson OFM Cap.
The Director
Anugraha, Nochiodaipatti
Dindigul East - 624003
Tamilnadu

Psychology in the area of Prenatal, Perinatal and Childhood is a fast emerging field. Professionals in medicine and psychology come together to focus on the earliest stages of human life-from preconception through infancy. Thirty years of worldwide clinical research supports the ancient Indian knowing that the beginning of life is the most important and impressionable. Psychological problems and illness start this early. Therefore, understanding what a baby really needs can form a protection against physical illness, mental illness, and suffering later in life.

A foetus learns intensely in the womb. One's earliest experiences imprint and become the subconscious programming. Prenatal- prenatal period is the time of building the foundations of a health body, emotions, and relationships. These established patterns are at the root of much health, relationship, emotional/ psychological and learning problems seen as all ages.

Over the years that I have practiced psychotherapy, many of my clients only got real relief from their pain when we worked on these early issues. I came to realize how difficult this was and how few adults would or could ever go this deep into themselves. At this point I began to think in terms of prevention. If parents could better understand what children need, and give it to them at the appropriate time, so much pain and illness could be prevented.

It is this view of psychology which Mrs. Kalyani is deeply committed to. The book "DHYAN BABY-a language for fetus", not only benefits from the author's empirical studies, it also gains from her academic and practical experience in conducting programmes for the pregnant women. Her experience as a therapist has contributed to her understanding of the prenatal care. During recent years, she has also been exposed to a wide number of clients which provided her with a good basis to engage in intense studies.

This book is enthusiastic celebration of motherhood and child upbringing. I think that this book will have numerous readers who will have gained a broader perspective of pregnancy and child upbringing. It explores the psychology of conception, pregnancy, delivery and the postpartum period, as well as the newborn child's intellectual and emotional development. There are signposts in these pages. Readers can use them to find their way to great treasures.

This book makes a remarkable contribution to the understanding of prenatal, prenatal period care. Academics, scholars, prospective or new parents, counselors and psychotherapists may all find this book stimulating. It also provides useful guidance for medical practitioners.

Best of luck to Mrs. Kalyani. God Bless! Wilson

FOREWORD

"All we are is the result of what we have thought. The mind is everything. What we think we become."- Buddha

It is true that the self talking is programming us and makes our statement to be true. Worldwide, the glory of positive thinking is being felt and strenuous efforts are being taken to learn it.

"What if the expectant mother assumes such kind of thinking, will it not affect the child?" –that was the question rose in our minds.

Further deep study of ancient Vedas, epics and books related to other religions reveal that really it is possible to enhance the intelligence of the baby when he/she is still in the mother's womb.

To our surprise, "Prenatal education", what we call this kind now, existed many years back.

Based on this Dhyan baby foundation was formed in the year 2004. For the past ten years many expectant mothers undertook such kind of prenatal programmes and have benefitted much.

This book is the result of the study and experience that we gained for the past ten years. Certainly, being the eye opener, this book will make positive impacts in the minds of expectant mothers all over the world.

It is not that prenatal education is the only the thing to have a gifted child! But, when it is good, why should we hesitate to add this good practice to our overall treasury of goodness?

Please come and be prepared for making better next generation and society!

-AUTHORS

1

MOTHERHOOD

It is rare to be born as human! It is still rare to be

born as woman!!. To such femininity, the one which brings glory is the motherhood. It is the highest, holiest service assumed by human kind.

Motherhood is the dream, and the ambition of every woman. Everybody aspires for happiest, healthy and fulfilled motherhood. Even, it is more important for every mother to have a healthy, beautiful, intelligent and long living child.

Is it possible to have all?

If a woman wishes…,

And, that too, if a pregnant woman wishes, yes, it is possible!

It is possible for the pregnant woman to change the world.

"THERE IS NO LIMIT TO WHAT A MOTHER CAN ACCOMPLISH. RIGHTEOUS WOMEN HAVE CHANGED THE COURSE OF HISTORY AND WILL CONTINUE TO DO SO." (By Julie B. Beck)

Yes, with certain practices, all are possible!

Such kinds of practices are being followed worldwide now a day. One of such practices is done at Dhyanbaby foundation(established in south India) through certain programme for pregnant women in which enriching baby's intellectuality is done when the baby is still in the womb. This is called as prenatal education.

"Enriching baby's intelligence in the womb itself?"

"What a strange thing it is!"

"Is it necessary?"

"Did intelligent people born like this before?"

Such questions may arise in your minds.

A small example...

Imagine a big and beautiful tree. Its branches are laden with beautiful flowers and tasteful fruits. The tree is thronged

with various kinds of tweeting, chirping and singing birds.

Besides, the tree provides cold shade along with gentle breeze!

Surely, every one of us would like to visit that place and wish to stay under the tree. You feel enthusiastic, even when you think of that tree and its majesty.

Now, do you know how the tree could grow so big and attain such fame?

It is all because of the roots which are out of our sight and hidden under the ground and other favorable conditions which provide continuous nourishments to the tree through the roots from its gestation period,

Like this, today, we admire the top performers in the mankind like Dr. A.P.J. Abdulkalam(former President of India), Mr Obama (US President), A.R. Rahman(Oscar winning musician), and Viswanathan Anandh(world "number one" chess player).

They are also human being like us. But, what had caused them to achieve a great success in their respective fields?

Just compare the roots explained in the above example. Like a root and other favorable conditions which are the bases for the tree, there exist some unseen things which are even not felt by the parents during the growing stage of the fetus. Some changes that had happened in the womb during the growth of the fetus might have been one of the reasons for the success of those top performers.

There would not be a big tree without a seed grown under certain favorable conditions!

In this field, we, at Dhyanbaby foundation, have done some research medically, psychologically and spiritually over several years and have found some relations between the cares taken by the pregnant women (especially psychological & spiritual cares) and Child's intelligence.

*****

2

FOUNDATION FOR HUMAN LIFE

We wish to build a luxurious house.

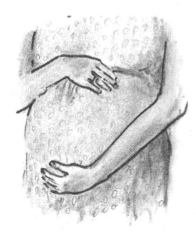

That house has to have a longstanding life of over several hundred years.

To achieve that, what should we do?

Yes, besides the selection of suitable place and other quality building materials, the important thing is to provide a strong foundation.

After the construction of the house, we cannot see the foundation. Everybody could see only the top parts of the buildings.

Our friends and relatives may appreciate our excellent taste and appropriate selection of good building materials, colour of the walls and other luxurious things, but they never would go in deep to check how strong the foundation is.

If we spend more money on luxurious things to get appreciation (most correctly 'Envy') from others and ignore spending money for the strong foundation, which is not visible and not attracting other's attention, who is going to lose?

The strength of the building will not go beyond the level of windows!

The improper foundation will result in decreased life of the buildings!!

Now, leave alone the foundation for building.

What is the foundation for the life of a human being who is going to live for hundred years?

The period of ten months in which the human beings stay as a fetus in mother's womb is the FOUNDATION for the mankind.

Ten months period in mothers' womb!

That is the foundation for the mankind.

How the mother pays attention for this period of ten months is imperative for the child to flourish in its life for the rest of hundred years!!

The baby may not be in mother's arms just yet, but that does not mean she and the child can't get to know each other and form a bond.

There is no other time in life where mother and baby is better able to communicate and share the most intimate feelings. In fact, there is no place for a pregnant mother to hide her emotions from her unborn child. The first school for every man or woman is his/her mother's womb. The greatest teacher is the expectant mother.

When the building collapses due to improper foundation, we will not be losing much. With additional investment we may rebuild the building using stronger foundation again.

But, just imagine!

After the birth of the baby, if we find that we have not given enough care during pregnancy period to improve the baby's intellectual qualities, is it possible for you to ask the baby to re-stay in the mother's womb for giving him / her proper foundation again?

Not possible!

Hence let us help the baby to learn important things useful to his/her life, when it is in the mother's womb, using programmes like done in Dhyanbaby foundation which have been evolved scientifically, psychologically and spiritually.

*****

3

SPIRITUALITY & SCIENCE IN MOTHERHOOD

Getting pregnant, taking care throughout the period of ten months and giving birth to a healthy baby, are not easy jobs.

Now, we witness boundless growth of science especially in the field of medicines.

But, it is bizarre that still there are many couples including doctors (!), longing for having a child!

They seem destined never to have the opportunity of having a baby!!

Let us discuss about this by viewing it in different angles.

"Marriages are fixed in the heaven" is the old saying.

Is somebody there in the heaven to confirm & fix our marriages?

Somebody would say that person in the heaven is our Lord Almighty.

Somebody would say that person is our ancestor! But, nobody can confirm whether it is Lord or our ancestor, as nobody has ever seen it!

However, according to Vedic and puranas, the reality is different. If you have happened to read the books like "The secret of Vedics" (or) spiritual in reality etc., you might have understood that the person in the heaven is actually the child to be born.

It is believed by vedics that the child from the heaven decides and selects its future parents.

Every Soul, according to its experiences that were gained in its previous births, selects it future parents in its reincarnation.

It is said that because of such strong desire of the soul, the marriages are happening for the couples not only among close relations, but beyond the countries belonging to different races, religion and languages.

Besides the above explanation, let us seek the logical reason scientifically.

The science says the world is made up of atoms.

Different atoms, according to their own frequencies and nature combine with other atoms of same frequencies to form land, water, sky, fire etc.

In the same way the soul – an invisible atom joins with the other atoms (of parents) of same frequency.

Whatever may be the logical reason, the motherhood is a wonderful thing! Is n't it?!

Some body may ask, why some couples are having baby immediately where as some couples take five years or ten years to have a baby and... for some couple there is no baby at all?

The reason may be that the baby would have expected more love & importance from the future parents.

Just imagine, if we have the baby after five years, how much importance & love we would give to that baby!

If the soul doesn't select some couples who are not having same frequencies, these couples will never have babies. The bible & vedas describe the marriage between these couples as "Toy- Marriage".

*****

4

IT IS A BOON TO HAVE A BABY

About five years back, I was in a famous hospital located in a big city practicing Dhyanbaby programme. The doctor of that hospital was a great scholar in gynecology and had done a good deal of research in the field of pregnancy.

After every Dhyan baby programme, she noticed much happiness in the faces of couples who had under taken the therapies from me. Then, with a curiosity, she requested me to allow her to attend one of such therapy programmes.

We had one such programme in the evening of that day itself. She attended that therapy programme.

She keenly asked many questions related to that therapy and understood the importance of it.

After the therapy, when I approached her, I was surprised to see her eyes welled with water.

"Tears! From the eyes of such great personality!?" I wondered.

I could not believe myself, as I had, from the morning, witnessed many couples thanking her for her great help in getting babies.

Almost everybody worshipped her.

"Mam! Why...?" I did not have enough strength to ask her further.

Her voice was shaky, Barely covering the sob that was about to break out, she kept her voice low and spoke slowly to relay a sense of steadiness, like the "calm before a storm of grief".

With a hoarse voice she replied,

"In order to understand the importance of mother hood, please convey my story to your clients...."

She paused for a moment and then clearing her throat continued to tell.

"It has been twenty years since my marriage. Even though we didn't have any physical abnormality (medically), we were destined from having a baby. For the first five years, I did not take it too serious. But, after that, I was longing for having a baby. When all other normal medical treatments failed, we opted for artificial insemination.

There are many practical difficulties with this method. Besides spending lots of money, with delicate medication and too much rest, our body & mind will be affected. If we fail to conceive two times with this method, the medical effects will be too serious after the age of forty. Even though we accepted to take all the risks, finally in my case, we could not succeed with this method."

She seemed regained from the sorrow.

Then she continued after a brief pause.

"Then we, after delegating our job & this hospital to our relative, went to London & America to learn new technique and skills in the field of pregnancy and childbirth. With those skills now we are helping the society. Those skills, learnt by us, were not useful for us to have a baby, and I didn't have the opportunity to feel and enjoy what the expectant mothers do. Still, sometimes, I am longing for that. Now, I am certain that whether it is through natural or artificial, unless the child decides we cannot become a mother. Having a child is such a great boon".

Finally that Doctor, with a sense of relief, appreciated me for doing such kind of programmes for the expectant mothers who have got the opportunity of becoming mothers out of many hurdles.

Next to getting pregnancy, she felt, it is very important to all expectant mothers to take care during the whole pregnancy period to have gifted children.

*****

5

CHILD'S EXPECTATION AS A FOETUS

Let us imagine the following scene like a cartoon film!

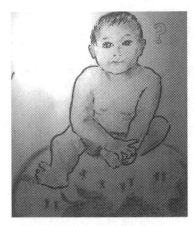

All the new couples in the world, raising their hands towards the sky, are calling a child to come to their family.

That child has too many choices. He has many options to select the right couple as his parents!

And, to select the right time to join them!

He may enter as another child to the family of Thirubai Ambani!(Founder of RELIANCE in India)... or To the family of Obama!.... Or to a scientist or to some loving family!

Even though that soul of child has so many choices in the wide world, now it has decided to come to you to see you as a mother & father and to do meditation (Dhyan) in the dark room of the mother's womb.....

Now, how are you going to thank that soul? How are you going to be trustful person to that child, because it has trusted you?

How wonderful experience it will be to become a mother and father!

In our Dhyan baby programmes, exercises are given to strengthen such a trust and bond between parents and child.

We should remember that during pregnancy the child not only gets energy from what the mother eats, but also gets all the emotions of her, such as happiness, sorrow, enthusiasm, worry, and anger etc. These emotional thoughts of the mother will affect the child in the womb.

Weird?!

Do you think so?

Let us see in detail.

Our body and mind are not different. Both are related to each other – one has adverse effect on other.

For example, "Fear" is one of the thoughts of mind. Heart is one of the parts of our body. When we suddenly encounter to see a cat in front of us, the fear will immediately catch hold of us.

What happens to the heart, at that time?

It starts to pound 140 times per minute instead of normal 72 times per minute. The emotional thought results in a "change" in the action of a body-part.

In the same way, the emotion of a pregnant woman affects the child which is also a part of mother's body as fetus. It is not a separate soul & body. If it is so, it should get the oxygen separately. It does not get oxygen through its noses by protruding it out of mother's belly... but, gets through mother's placenta.

That is why whatever changes happening to mother's body will affect the baby.

In our house, if we want to hide the strife between the couples from our grown-up child, we can keep the child in a separate room and continue our fight in another room.

But is it possible when the baby is inside mother's womb?

For the whole period of ten months, the baby is with the mother. Every moment, it enjoys and experiences whatever the mother is doing like breathing, eating, seeing, hearing etc. In such case, is it possible for us to hide our other feelings from the child?

No, certainly not possible!

All the feelings will also be observed & absorbed by the baby.

Hence, it is very important duty for every expectant mother to do everything good. In this way we are showing our trust & love to the child in return to its initial trust. One of such good things is to undergo Dhyan baby programme- a prenatal education!

*****

6

A PRENATAL EDUCATION AND THERAPY
(DHYAN BABY PROGRAMME)

Need for pre natal education

"**P**revention is better than cure" is an old adage. And, it is true forever!

Consider a computer!

Don't we find it easy to protect the computers by installing a FIRE WALL, rather than letting viruses inside the computer and struggling to clean them up later?!

In fact, our ancient India had strong ethically based education system (the greatest FIRE WALL), which impart strong ethics into human minds and pave way for a healthy and good society with strong bonds. It was said that, when the British attempted to pervade India, the first thing they understood and did was to abolish our education system.

Japanese, after their complete destruction by the attacks of nuclear bombs, revived through strong education system. The foremost thing they did after the collapse was to inculcate strong ethical values in to the minds of younger generation (from infant stage).

Result?!

The samurai became the great citizen and now the Japan is ruling the world economically!

After letting go of our strong education systems, now, we are lamenting about secularism, terrorism, scandals, etc., in our country, India. Not coping with these environments, people have been caught into the vicious holds of stress and have fallen as prey to it!

We know, of course, it will be still better to protect the computer by "not down loading unnecessary programmes or not visiting some dangerous /restricted sites".

Even though we pay more attention in protecting our computers, but, when it comes to us, the human being who is a very complicated and mega computer, we are so reluctant to apply the same principle,

After letting in all sorts of viruses into our minds, now, we have started talking about ethical education systems and are showing interest to establish ethical labs to eradicate these viruses. We are now convinced (again) that ethics have to be taught as early as possible.

Haven't our great puranas and epics taught us before?

We have treasure of knowledge and wisdom in our ancient epics, which are proved again now.

Our ancestors knew that the good education starts right from the mother's womb.

We are still having unanswered questions of why the children from the same parents behave differently or become persons having entirely contradicting characters.

If it is genes, as the science believes, which decide the character and transfer it hereditarily, then, how come the possibility of having children of different characters from the same parent?

Some other things are also there for this disparity.

One of the ways to eliminate this disparity and form a good society and thereby a good nation is through early education. And that too through pre natal education! We are not saying that prenatal education is the only the other thing! But, when it is good, why should we hesitate to add this good practice to our overall treasury of goodness?

*****

7

ABOUT NEURONS AND LORD KRISHNA'S ILLUSTRATION

From the fourth month, the brain's growth becomes fast so as to form about 2,50,000 neurons per minute. The total no. of neurons at birth is equal to that of an adult.

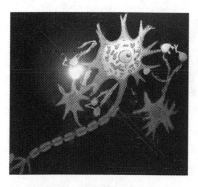

Then, why that child is not having enough wisdom that an adult has?

Wisdom is nothing but the connections between the neurons. Each neuron has about 10,000 connections with adjacent neurons.

The highly congested network in the world!

The connection between neurons is formed by the wisdom got through the learning process in which it receives many lessons through external & internal stimuli.

Un- connected neurons won't make any harm to us as 50% of connections are enough for our human programme. It has been proved scientifically that making connection between neurons at later age is very difficult.

So, it is in the hands of parents to assist the child to use its all neurons effectively.

We are now talking about neurons based on so many scientific researches, but can you believe me, if I say, Lord Krishna has told this to Arjuna so many years back.

How? Let us see now!

 During kurushetra war, Lord Krishna was driving the horse car for Arjuna. Kourawas, the enemy of Arjuna, at that time, laid a "Chakra Vyuha" (a circular grid like defense arrangement) to the shock of Arjuna.

The Chakra Vyuha, as shown in the figure, was very difficult to penetrate. Because of this arrangement the attacker is not able to focus on a "still target" in front as the targets keep changing with the rotation of the chakras (circle like wheels). Even if the attacker somehow manages to penetrate one ring, the rotating nature of the Vyuha makes sure that the ring he has penetrated closes behind him causing the attacker to be trapped within the Chakravyuha.

Arjuna, bewildered with the enemy's arrangement, asked Lord Krishna, "Krishna!, only three persons, you, Lord Sooriya(sun) and me know the secret of breaking into and getting back from the chakra Vyuha. But, I have to be here to save the army of my brother, then, whom do we trust and send to break the Chakra Vyuha?"

Lord Krishna replied calmly, "Send your son Abhimanyu!"

Surprised by Krishna's answer, Arjuna asked back. "Krishna! Even though I know the secret of Chakra vyuha, actually I did not have enough time to teach my son, as I was engaged in various activities like Vanavasa (living in the forest), Agnanavasa (living hideously) etc. How can I send my son, who doesn't know the secret?"

Krishna firmly looked into the eyes of Arjuna and replied him with a smile,

"Arjuna! I already taught him the secret"

Arjuna knew that when Krishna taught him the secret of that Vyuha, his son, Abhimanyu was yet to born. After that Krishna had also been always with him and his brothers.

"How did he find time to teach my son?" Arjuna wondered.

Krishna noticing his doubtful face recalled the old incidence. "Arjuna! When I was explaining the secret of Chakravyuha to you, your son also heard from the womb of his mother Subhadhra. So, don't worry, he can go". Krishna assuaged Arjuna's fears.

Arjuna could not believe that a fetus could hear and learn.

He requested Krishna to explain further.

"Listen, Arjuna," Krishna started to explain, "A child's brain in the womb is so receptive that it can absorb more deeply any word or deed even when the child hear or experience it by one time. It is almost equal to learning through millions of repetitions after the birth."

That was the illustration by Lord Krishna about the greatest absorption power of child when it is still in its mother's womb.

However, later during the Mahabharata War, Abhimanyu easily got into the Chakravyuha but he failed to return back as he was unaware of the way to come out from it.

The reason for his failure was explained in the story of Mahabharatha as below.

Krishna was narrating his experience with the technique of Chakravyuha to both Arjuna and Subhadhra (sister of Krishna). The technique was so complicated that it involved many step by step procedures for entering into the circles. Nonetheless, when Krishna was explaining seventh step, Subhadra did not find the topic interesting and she soon fell asleep.

Abhimanyu who had been so far hearing the techniques from his mother's womb also dozed off.

The unfortunate Abhimanyu could never obtain the technique of breaking circles beyond the seventh one in the chakra-vyuha, but whatever he had heard Sri Krishna say, he carefully preserved in his memory. Despite his incomplete knowledge of the technique he entered the grid and overcame one circle after another until he came to the seventh one, the breaking of which he had no knowledge. Even though he was so brave and ambitious, all his efforts to win became vain. His strength and bravery proved no match against the skillfully laid out maze of warriors and finally he met his end.

This story highlights the importance of the first 3 sanskaras and how the healthy mental growth of a child begins even before it is born, while still in its mother's womb. Recent scientific findings have shown that babies can indeed hear from inside their mother.

Hence, today's explanation through scientific research about the neurons & its connections coincides with Lord Krishna's explanation.

What a wonderful absorption power of fetus!

*****

8

CONCEPTUAL PERIOD

In our Indian Country, our ancestors have devised each activity with a meaning, after an extensive research.

From fixing of date & time for the marriage to fixing auspicious time for honeymoon, all are selected cautiously in order to deliver a great soul with a healthy body and mind.

Today's scientists also accept the impact of date, time, and crescent moon on our lives.

The advice to the couples to follow certain things during conception period scientifically and spiritually is nothing but to keep their mind and body clean, calm and healthy. There is also an insistence from therapists to have particular light, color, aroma in the honey moon room. Color, aroma and light therapies give guidelines for that.

So, it is our duty to follow what our ancestors had taught us, of course, at the same time following modern scientific ways. It is to give the world the best child.

CONCEPTION TO BIRTH (PRENATAL DEVELOPMENT)

The overall period from conception to birth is 40 weeks. Within this period, the development occurs in three stages. In biological terms we call them as GERMINAL, EMBRYONIC and FETAL.

The first two stages last for about 9 weeks. The third stage as fetus starts from 9th week and ends at birth. After birth, the fetus becomes child.

During the germinal stage of prenatal development, the cells necessary for the placenta, umbilical cord, and amniotic fluid will differentiate to form the embryo. The size of the embryo will be around two inches.

The neural tube is formed first in this period. This will become the spinal cord and brain. As the nervous system starts to develop, the tiny heart starts to pump blood. The stage has fastest growth as all organs such as digestive tract, back bone, intestines, eyes, nose, ears and jaws grow fast.

However, as the embryo is so tiny, it is susceptible to get damaged due to outside influences resulting in abortion. Mothers should take much care in this period.

Now comes to fetal stage.

During this period the development of remainder continues, but at much slower pace.

Apart from growth of individual organs, the arms and legs start to move.

The mother can feel and find its movements.

Brain growth during this period allows the fetus to develop new behaviors.

The fetus becomes sensitive to light and sound. When strong light rays fall on the belly of mother, the baby will attempt to shield its eyes.

Towards the period of birth, the brain grows even rapidly. The outer side of the brain called Cerebral cortex grows larger and the fetus spends more hours awake.

The neural connections in the brain are started. And as such, the fetus moves with more coordination.

After around 28 weeks, the thalamus which is below the brain starts to form and allow the brain to be connected with sensory organs like ears and eye. In this stage, the personality begins to emerge. The fetus can distinguish between voices, remember songs and certain sounds after birth.

So, when a child becomes fetus itself, its color, character, intelligence, wisdom, courage, prowess, confidence etc., are formed during first half of the conceptual period.

Balance 50% continues to form during full of pregnancy period by absorbing whatever we give internally and externally.

It is very important to have good mind and healthy body during the initial conceptual period in which the second 50% of all characters are formed. The personality of the child depends upon the healthy levels of mind & body of the couples during the conceptual period. Hence, it is imperative to teach the techniques &practices of "how to keep the mind & body well" to the new couples & to those who are waiting to have baby.

*****

9

PARENT'S MOOD AND ITS IMPACT ON THE CHILD

When a couple unites their minds together for the child, the child is born based on their moods.

We are having excellent examples as stories in our "Mahabharatha". Let us see one of them.

The story is about the birth of Dhirutharashtra, Pandu and Vidhura.

When the saint as well as emperor Vyasar gifted Ambikai and Ambalikai (his two queens) the "child – bearing – benediction" through "Nayoga energy", Ambikai closed her eyes on seeing the horrific figure of the rishi(the saint) which he attained through weariness when he wandered in the forest for meditation.

Ambalikai, feared and sweated.

Later, Vyasar explained to his mother Sathyavathi who was also the mother-in-law for both Ambikai and Ambalikai that they would have babies depending upon the mood and as such Ambikai would have blind-baby and Ambalikai would have a baby with "leucoderma-skin with white patches".

Sathayawathi was much worried about these children & wondered how to make these heirs to be crown as the kings for Hasthinapura.

Hence, she approached Ambikai to give another opportunity of delivering a baby with all excellent qualities and requested her to go to Viyasar with a good mind & happiness.

As Ambikai did not like this, she made her lady-servant, Vadhalikai, to go under the camouflage of her. Having well known about Vyasar, the re- incarnation of Lord and his wisdom, Vadhalikai with good mind & happiness united with Vyasar.

As a result of this, a child of good mind & body, with a power to establish virtue and justice was born.

He was Vidhurar!

The above story clearly explains the impact of moods of parents during conceptual period, even though so many other stories & dissertations are there on the above subject.

Even doctors recommend that a woman must be physically and mentally healthy during her pregnancy period.

Doctors say that a mother's mental state reaches her fetus. During a recent research, two non-native English s p e a k i n g e x p e c t a n t mothers were asked to listen to English audio tapes. One lady was given an audio tape with American accent while the other lady was given the one with British accent.

When their children were around 4 years old, their English knowledge was remarkable with the respective accents even though they were not native English speakers.

You might have known that the Japanese and Chinese would find it very difficult to speak English. One of the reasons is that they don't have the letter 'L' in their native script and so they can't pronounce it. For example they will pronounce the word 'follow' as 'forrow' in spite of giving them a lot of training.

Again, the research has proved that they could grasp it only if they were trained when they were below three years of age. After that they could not grasp the letter 'L' irrespective of the intensity of the training. The grown child is not able to absorb it into its system.

That is why a mother's relationship with her unborn child is both extraordinary and amazingly powerful.

Scientifically it has been proved that the baby listen to the heartbeat of its mother and her voice. It is also responding to the music during its stay in the womb. So similarly it can be able to identify a mantra or a story repeated by its mother.

Actually, such practices enhance the concentration and listening skills of the child.

So, as per the advices by our ancestors, doctors and scientists, the "would be parents" should have good mood during conceptual period. In that period one should not eat more food, should avoid digestion disorders and take care to keep body, intestine, etc. very clean.

*****

10

MYSTERY OF OUR BODY

It is a great wonder how a big body is formed from a single cell. Also during our birth, our weight is around 3 to 3.5 Kg. At that time, we have all the limbs that an adult have, like eyes, hands, legs etc., but of small size.

As we grow, all the limbs also grow proportionally. But, no new limb is formed during our growth other than what we had during our birth.

Did we have a second nose or third eye, during our growth? No.

But, when comes to neurons of our brain, they are formed fully before the birth. At birth its number is almost equivalent to that of an adult. We cannot add new neurons afterwards. But, the absorption power & perception power of such neurons can be developed later on stage.

Nonetheless, the best stage to lay foundation for developing the absorption & perception powers is the fetus stage.

Like many prenatal education programmes around the world, the Dhyan baby programme also has been so devised to give such power to the fetus to learn new behaviors and knowledge step by step in every month of pregnancy period.

*****

11

GENES, GENES, GENES!

Even though we have good mood, and try to hear good things, see good things during the pregnancy period for the good development of child, what about the impact of genes?"

This type of question may arise in the minds of you.

For example someone may ask, "My mother, has 'sugar' and 'high blood pressure', so, isn't quite natural that, I also should inherit such diseases through genes?"

Now, shall we answer for another question?

"Suppose, you are a plant of yielding "red flowers" and your husband is also the same kind of plant, then, what kind of sapling do you expect out of both of you?"

You may answer must be 'Red-flower plant'.

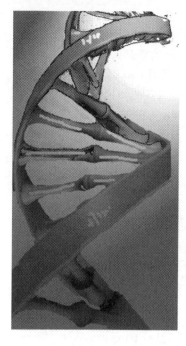

Now, is it possible to make the sapling, after its growth, to yield different color of flowers?'

It is impossible!

However, when it is growing, if we do the process of 'hybrid', that is, crossbreeding it with another plant of "white-color", the resultant sapling will yield pink color flowers.

If more 'white color plants' are inter crossed with that plant, then almost we can more number of white color saplings.

Normally, the disease from the parents is transferred through heredity to the infants. Especially, the HIV affected parents will have HIV kids. But, with the advent of today's medical technology & intensive research on the absorption & adaptation of the fetus, if the HIV affected mother takes proper medicine, good & healthy child will be born.

For this advancement in technology, stem cells and life cells play important roles. If we take some of the stem cells during the birth of a baby and preserve it, even after 30 years we can re-use it to alleviate most of the diseases. That is the wonderful power of stem cells! If such is the case, please think what will be the power of stem cells when they are at the womb.

So, if we properly utilize these cells, healthy children will be born even to ill-health parents.

Now, have you ever wondered when you happened to see a baby behaving like her mother even though the mother was not with the baby for quite a long time?

It is because of the genes!

If you can see tendencies that seem to emerge in different generations and branches of the family, there is a good chance that these have a strong genetic component. The genes that contain these genetic components are found inside the nucleus of every cell. They consist, a set of instructions to make enzymes which enable the cells to function properly.

Human mostly inherits the same basic set of genes, although there are some small variations in the structure of each gene. In fact, these inherited variations can result in considerable differences in the way the brains of different individual function.

Even though, the overall character—the personality— of the human being is shaped by many different influences through life, the biological component of personality, known as temperament, is present from the birth. The temperament is the person's nature as it affects the way he or she thinks, feels and behaves.

In each one of our families, it will be no wonder to find that each child seem to develop unique personalities from a very early age, despite growing up in a very similar environment.

It has been found that the physical characteristics like eye color, etc., are determined by several genes. The same holds true for personality characteristics too. In addition to genes, the behavior characteristics are influenced by other environmental factors such as parenting, education, lifestyle, diet, etc.

Suppose a man who inherits genes that make him susceptible to depression may indeed become depressed, but the influence of good parenting, education, etc., may well protect the person.

If we utilize the pregnant period properly, we can have the same children what we wanted during the pregnant period.

*****

12

ABOUT OUR BRAIN AND CONSCIOUSNESS

As we have seen in the previous chapters the brain is the fastest growing organ in the body. While all other organs take years together to grow, the brain cells are produced up to a quarter of a million every minute in a developing fetus. At birth a baby's brain contains as many nerve (neuron) cells as it will have as an adult.

It has been revealed by scientists that the neurons start to connect each other after birth which we can literally mean a "growth".

Actually these neural connections are otherwise called "wisdom". Even at birth, few neural connections have been found. It has been proved that the sensory activity is the source of such neural connections.

In our Thirukkural, the great poet Valluvar has also said that the wisdom improves through continuous learning as like water gushing in the well on digging deeply. The wisdom can be otherwise called as "consciousness".

Consciousness is the most remarkable product of the human brain. It is the medium for our thoughts and gives meaning to our experiences. Without it we could not experience sight or sound, taste, touch or smell. Unfortunately no single definition is there for consciousness as it is multifaceted. Still the riddle of consciousness is yet to be solved by experts.

Even though there are many theories, they all accept one point that consciousness has to involve the integration activity from several brain net works, allowing us to perceive our surroundings as one single unifying experience rather than isolated sensory perceptions.

Whatever may be the theory, the consciousness is the pool of experiences gained over a period of millions of years and it is evolutionarily being passed on to next generation.

We need not go deeply into it as there are still many unanswered questions.

What we have to understand is that our wisdom depends upon what we input through our sensory organs. If we understand clearly about the development of sensory organs in the womb, then we will be convinced about the necessity of prenatal education.

*****

13

Formation of sensory organs and how to train them?

TOUCH:

This is the first sense we use.

The fetus experiences its surroundings through contact with the walls of the maternal womb. The touching sense is also the very first means of communication with outside world. There are on average fifty receptors per square millimeter of our skin. But they are unevenly distributed. Our way of experiencing touch and interacting physically with others is rooted in our early sensations of life in the Uterus.

SOUND:

Hearing is the second sense to be aroused in the fetus which can hear noises and recognize some low sounds in Uterus.

SMELL:

Chronologically this is the third sense to enter our life. At birth, a baby is already able to recognize its mother's smell.

TASTE:

Taste buds start to develop around seventh week. Most taste buds arise on the tongue. Each barrel shape bud has free ends having receptive gustatory hairs. This sense of taste uses some 10,000 taste buds in our mouth. Studies indicate that the flavors and aromas of the foods mom eats during pregnancy, which pass through to her amniotic fluid, may affect her baby's taste preferences long after birth

SIGHT:

By the sixth month visual cells (photo receptive rods and cones), bipolar cells and ganglion cells (which sprout axons that grow back through the optic stalk and make connections within the brain) are formed. Our brain receives 80% of its information from the sense of sight, even though it is the least developed of the sense in the babies.

So the basic senses are almost formed during the period in the womb and depending upon the feed through these sense organs some neural connections are formed.

We might have heard that people learn and perceive things differently.

There are basically four categories of people.

1) Those people who learn only through seeing,

2) Those, who learn only through hearing,

3) Those, who learn only through touching and

4) Those, who learn only through feeling.

This may be due to the reason that during their early life in their mother's womb a particular sense organ might have been stimulated. Again, if all the organs are finely honed and sharpened, their worldly perception will be entirely different.

Now, let us examine the following incidence of a story.

PERCEPTION THROUGH SENSES:

"It is like a rope" one man says.

"No, it is like a tree branch" says another man.

"You both are wrong! It is like a hand fan! ", declares the third man.

"Why all of you are struggling to perceive it correctly", says the fourth man, "it is like a wall!"

"Ha, ha", controlling his laugh with great difficulty says the fifth person; "It is like a solid pipe! Can't you feel it, you idiots!?"

"I don't think so! It is like a pillar" says the sixth person.

What is it, really? What they are all talking about?

Have you heard the story of six blind men and an elephant?

This story was originated in India. The six blind men were asked to determine what an elephant looked like by feeling different parts of elephant's body.

The first man touched the tail of the elephant.

The second man touched the trunk. The others touched different parts of the elephant's body like, the third one, the ear...the fourth one, the belly...the fifth one the tusk and the sixth one the legs of the elephant.

Now, one may wonder, "Who is correct?"

The verdict is that everyone was correct as per the data received by them. We may apply the moral of this story to various situations and may infer that each human being has his own belief system and the conflicts arise when they don't accept each other. If they understand the real truth, then, there will be no conflict.

Now, we may look at this story in another angle in which we may consider the six blind men as the six senses of a human being.

If, he, using his all senses, fails to perceive the things around the world correctly, then he may have biased opinion about that particular thing and his response and actions towards it will be entirely different.

How to perceive the things correctly?

This could be done by tactfully applying all the senses that we have, to the particular situation when we analyze a thing.

Apart from traditionally known five senses like, seeing, hearing, tasting, smelling and touching, scientists are adding up more senses recently. They are, for example, nociception (pain), equilibrioception (balance), proprioception and kinaesthesia (joint motions and acceleration), sense of time, thermoception (temperature differences), agnetoception (direction),intuition, etc.

The point here is how are we going to use all the senses?

Practice makes a man perfect!

Only through practice and constant training!!

Hence, if we had practiced the right way of using all senses, automatically most of the senses will be simultaneously applied while we attempt to perceive things. Ultimately our perception will be very close to the truth.

If we could perceive the things around us perfectly, we can lead a harmonious and happy life. Success will always be there by our side!

Right time to train the senses

When is the right time to train our senses?

Scientists have proved that, the training of senses starts from earlier age, as Mr. Eric Berne, the greatest psychiatrist, puts on "the fate of a person is already decided by his learning process up to the first six years".

Our epics and puranas even went into one level up by saying that the learning process starts from the mother's womb. Now, science proves this theory through so many experiments and the age old theory is accepted again.

The science says that touching sense is formed first during 10 weeks of conception followed by tasting, smelling, hearing and seeing senses.

Hence, the mother, the first and the best teacher, can assist her baby to learn the practice of using senses while the sensing organs are formed. So, let us be ready to assist our babies to sharpen their senses from the womb itself!

*****

14

WILL THE FETUS LEARN?

Why do we have to teach a fetus?

Will the fetus in the womb receive any kind of education we impart?

Definitely!

As explained before, the pregnancy period is the only period where the mother spends every single second in a day with her baby and also this is the only period where the fetus absorbs every single input 100% without distractions.

Now consider the analogy between a Clay pot and shaping up the fetus.

When you are making a clay pot, its shape can be determined only when the clay is wet.

Once made and dried, the shape of the pot cannot be changed. If you try, it will break.

Similarly, you can shape up the IQ, EQ, SQ and whatever you want of a baby when it is in the womb. After birth it is similar to a dried pot.

Characters can be shaped or fine-tuned with the hard efforts of the expectant mother. The ten months the baby spends in the womb is the best period to train it for anything.

LEARNING THROUGH HEARING

Actually the womb is not exactly the quietest place for the baby to hang out. The baby not only hears the sounds that the mother makes – her stomach growling, hiccups or burps, but also the outside sounds like music, starting of a car, etc., The baby as a fetus will react to all the sounds by kicking or shifting around.

However, the fetus predominantly hears the sound made by the mother. It has been found that, around seventh month, a fetus's heart rate slows down slightly whenever his mother is speaking. This indicates that the mother's voice has calming effect on the fetus. By the time they are born, babies can actually recognize their mother's voices.

In Columbia University's college of physicians and surgeons, one study was conducted to find whether the fetus can recognize mother's voice after the birth.

In that study the doctors gave the infants pacifiers that were connected to tape recorders. Depending upon the sucking patterns, the pacifier would switch on either the tape recorder where mother's voice had been recorded or the other tape recorder where other woman's voice had been recorded.

To the amusement of the doctors, the infant could learn the correct sucking pattern within twenty minutes to switch the tape recorder of his mother's voice.

Other researches reveal that babies had first lessons in their native language while still in the womb. They all suck more vigorously to turn on the tape recordings of other people speaking in the same language what their mother used.

These studies suggest that the developing fetus gets all the information he need just by hearing his mother's conversations with others, or mother reading a book loudly.

LEARNING BY SEEING

Until seventh month period the baby's eyes are closed. After they open, the fetus is able to see. However, he could see only the darkness inside the womb. Whenever the mother goes outside and allows bright light to fall on her belly, the fetus can see it and even could react to evade the bright light.

Studies with ultra sound, proves that fetuses gradually open and close eyes more and more as the delivery neared. It was inferred that the fetus is practicing for blinking and seeing in the outside world.

Here, the mother can assist the fetus to learn to use the eyes perfectly.

LEARNING BY TASTING

The quality of food eaten by the mother is more important. The fetus also tastes the food what the mother has eaten. The fetus uses his taste to explore around the womb. There is some evidence that he can taste bitter, sweet, or sour flavours in the amniotic fluid.

Some ultra sound studies have shown that fetuses lick the placenta and uterine wall.

"The more varied a mother's diet during pregnancy and breastfeeding, the more likely that the infant will accept a new food," says Julie Mennella, Ph.D., biopsychologist at the Monell Chemical Senses Center, in Philadelphia.

LEARNING THROUGH SMELLING

As the fetus has used his smelling sensory organ inside the womb, for a few hours after birth he uses the sense of smell rather than his vision to identify his mother.

So, if the fetus had been trained perfectly in the womb to differentiate all the smells, it will be much useful for their entire life.

All this goes to show that a baby isn't just passively waiting to be born while in the womb. He's already building important skills and developing a strong bond with one of the most important people in his life—his mother.

The fast developing neurons of the brain yearn to absorb any information that comes by its way. The science now starts to reveal that this is the best period for giving any kind of input and shaping the future of the baby after birth.

The unutilized neuron cells are all wasted. Now it is up to the expectant mother to decide whether to utilize the baby's cells fully or to waste them. The mother's continuous efforts in giving positive inputs to the fetus are much important. So finally it remains in the mother's hands whether she wants to make use of such a wonderful period and give a magnificent baby to this society and the world.

*****

15

INTELLIGENCE DEVELOPMENT

INTELLIGENT QUOTIENT-IQ

To assess the intelligence, the psychologists over a very long period, have designed many tests and the scores derived from the tests are expressed as IQ (Intelligent Quotient). The IQ of average person is around hundred.

There are so many influencing factors that affect IQ level. It starts from maternal (fetal) environment, family environment and to the genes and the health.

The children who are having IQ level more than hundred are called "Gifted Children".

Who else doesn't want to have Gifted Children?

But, to have Gifted Children, Have we taken any effort?

Besides good nutrition, good environments, the script taught by a mother to the fetus is also said to be one of the influencing factors for IQ improvement.

If a mother forms a strong bond during maternity, it continues to be strong even after birth and this bond results in good family environment for the child to develop still more IQ level.

EMOTIONAL QUOTIENT: EQ

One may wonder if I say you cannot be able to make your hands enter into a vessel having a bigger mouth!

But it is true!

When we are in haste, even a vessel, like a vat, with a mouth ten times larger than our hands' thickness is not enough for our hand to freely enter into it without touching the walls!

Which is inhibiting our ability?

Of course, it is the haste, the result of bad emotions, which is inhibiting our ability to make our hands to enter into the vessel without touching its walls! Haste makes waste!

If we are emotionally intelligent, we will take stock of the situation rightly and patiently handle the situation. Emotional intelligence is the ability to identify, assess and control the emotions of oneself, of others and of groups.

The emotionally intelligent person can capitalize fully upon his changing moods in order to best fit the task at hand. We are judged by not how smart we are, but, also by how well we handle each other and ourselves. If we are emotionally bankrupt, any level of intelligence will be of no use for our rescue!

We are seeing many temporarily successful persons ending their lives in hospitals not coping with environmental demands and pressures.

There are many schools of thoughts about emotional intelligence. Most of the scientists accept that it is an in-born character and nurtured and further programmed up to the first six years of our life. Again and again, it is being proved that the parents' contribution, especially the mother's, is crucial for the successful life of the child.

All the religions insist the important role of mother when she is in conception.

The awareness, stress tolerance, problem solving, happiness, coping with environmental demands and pressures, etc., are said to be learnt by the fetus in the womb, not verbally but emotionally.

The emotional quotient (EQ) develops during the seventh month.

Is EQ really important?

Definitely!

Because not all intellectuals are stress free, happy and content without tension.

But is this an appropriate time to give this therapy?

When we give some information to a twenty five years old man, and boys of ten years old and three years old, who do you think will grasp faster?

All of us will agree that the three year old will grasp the information fast.

Then imagine someone younger than the three years old. When a baby is born, he/ she has about hundred crore neurons(one billion). These neurons are equivalent to the intellectual cells of a grown up person. Up to the age of three, the baby's receiving capacity is very high and will absorb any training given to him/her.

If this is the case for a growing child, imagine the capacity of a fetus. Once a baby is born all the developed cells only grow in size, we have not heard of a new organ being formed after birth. During pregnancy, a new cell is formed every second with the fetus. So at this time we can feed the fetus with rich thoughts, intelligence and actions.

There are many infant related stories from ancient times to the present days.

The story of Bhakta Prahalatha is a perfect example.

His mother fed him with stories of Narayanapuranam(epic of Lord Sri Narayana) so he could be born as a pious baby. In fact, he is the one to have earned the name as 'GarbaSreeman' (The person who learned in the womb), because he learned a lot when he was in his mother's womb. So the technique of teaching the fetus was followed even during ancient times.

Keeping this in mind we, at Dhyan baby foundation, give therapies according to the mother's mind set. We have been seeing how a mother's emotional state of mind affects her fetus.

In an interview, the South Indian Tamil actor Kamal Hassan mentioned that when his mother was expecting the birth of his elder brother Charu Hassan, she was totally pre-occupied in litigation activities. This made her spending a lot of time in the court. The imprints were passed on to her foetus and today Kamal Hassan's brother is an advocate.

Similarly, when his mother was pregnant with him, she watched a lot of movies and visited shooting spots. This effect rubbed on to Kamal Hassan and today as all of you know, Kamal is a great actor.

Even India's Ex-President Dr Abdul Kalam's brother commented that when his mother was pregnant with Abdul Kalam, she was radiating with energy and brightness. So they were aware and expecting Abdul Kalam to be an intellectual and well-read scholar.

From ancient times to the present times, irrespective of caste, creed, culture, tradition, religion and geographic region, everyone gives immense importance to the pregnancy period.

SPIRTUAL QUOTIENT (SQ):

So long as we blame outside sources, our miseries will continue and we will feel helpless. All religions have been teaching us about the inward journey to discover the essence of our being, to harness our mind and to channelize all our energy for great performance.

Knowing about the religion and doing some rituals will not yield a good spiritual enlightenment. But if the knowledge is transferred into wisdom, we will get enlightenment.

Many studies have revealed that the spirituality being followed during pregnancy period helps the fetus to learn the spiritual things emotionally. In all of our Indian epics and puranas, the necessity of following spirituality during pregnancy has been insisted.

For example, a research conducted in a big corporate firm found that at the entry level, the IQs of all employees were at the same level.

However only some persons could pass the second level test which measured their level of EQ. Travelling beyond this, persons in the core team had to have a high degree of SQ.

Recent researches prove that the IQ, EQ and SQ levels were developed in the womb itself.

Scientists have also proved that people who have high IQ may not necessarily have high EQ or SQ. It is similar for people who have a high level of EQ. But it has been proved that persons who have a high level of SQ also have a high level of IQ and EQ.

This SQ develops during the eighth month of pregnancy period.

CREATIVITY:

When Archimedes stepped into a bath and noticed that the water level rose, he suddenly understood that the volume of water displaced must be equal to the volume of the part of his body he had submerged.

He found the principle of measuring density of matters of irregular volume!

Another scientist, Sir Isaac Newton created the laws of gravity when an apple fell on his head as he sat in contemplative mood.

Why should the apple always descend perpendicularly to the ground, thought he himself!

Why should it not go sideways or upwards, but constantly to the earth's centre?

From this he concluded prudently that matter draws another matter proportional to the quantity. If the apple is bigger than earth, earth would have been drawn towards the apple!

But, these thinking did not occur to so many numbers of people who witnessed many apple falls or who had taken bath in the bath tubs many times!

Geniuses, who can apparently conjure these "sideways leaps of thought from thin air", say that they cannot pinpoint their source of inspiration.

So, what goes on in a brain when it makes such conclusion?

How distinct is inspiration from ordinary problem- solving?

From early childhood, we are encouraged to be creative - to use our imagination and discover innovative solutions (such as listing within three minutes as many uses as you can for a brick, book, etc.)

The short answer from psychologists is that creativity increases when we relax our grip on established ways of thinking and free our minds.

However, as Mr. Eric Berne puts on, if the mother writes a wrong script from the pregnancy period to earlier age of up to six years, it will become a curse and inhibit the child from attaining the above status!

So, it is in the hands of mother to help her child to become creative genius!

The mother can learn to help her child to attain balanced mind during pregnant period through proper tools.

IMPRINTS

There is a story about an eagle who laid eggs in a crow's nest. The baby eagle grew up with the crow's family thinking that he too was a crow.....

......and ...the rest of the story dealt with how the baby eagle realised about its own identity after so many struggles.

Here, what we have to understand is about the «imprint» that the crow had given to the baby eagle when the baby eagle first opened his eyes in the crow's nest!

It saw the face of the crow and the imprint of crow as his mother strongly instilled into its mind!

This has been proved, recently, through many scientific experiments. The results showed that the behaviours of animals change when they first open their eyes in another kind of animal's nest or place and grow with those kind of animals.

What are gene imprints? How do a mother's actions, thoughts and vision affect the fetus?

Let's recall an article that appeared in the newspapers about some years ago. A black baby was born to a white German couple. The whole world was wondering how a black baby can be born to a white couple though DNA tests proved that the baby was born to them.

Scientists went into a dizzy of research with the fact that starting seven generations before there was no black from both the families. Then, how did they have a black baby?

They realized that it was due to the mother's imprints.

During her pregnancy period, the lady visited many orphanages to spend time with little children. She had developed great affinity with black children. Whenever she interacted with black children, she used to wholeheartedly enjoy seeing them, interacting with them, listening to them, etc. This was done with great involvement. Moreover, she hung a picture of a black baby in her room. During her leisure time she used to see the baby with great passion.

Scientists after a lot of research have proved that a black baby was born to her because of the great affinity she showed towards them during her pregnancy. This event proves that imprints of vision do reach the fetus.

Not only the science, but our ancient vedics also taught us about the importance of imprints during pregnant period.

Don't we get advices from our older people not to see or hear about bad things during pregnant period?

In the vedics of Garpini raksha, rules have been laid even on "how to offer gifts to a pregnant lady" as below.

"When offering gifts to a pregnant lady, like dresses, ornaments, etc., care should be taken that they are of holistic, clean and fresh, unbroken, unbreakable and likable by her."

See, even the imprints of broken or unsuitable gifts have strong influence on the growth of a baby!

If at all, when the mother has to face unfavorable situations, the other handy solutions are there for her help. They can be easily attainable and obtainable through proper procedures and mind exercises.

Making a good soul is the number one karma (deed) in our life.

Based on this concept, some specific therapies are there to enhance the intellectual power of the baby.

Recently, a couple approached the author of this book with a valid doubt. They told her that both of them were short tempered and one of their genes carried a chronic disease. They were wondering whether through some therapies, the negative trait could be stopped from passing on to their child.

The author assured them that whether they take some therapies or not, but, whatever a mother does during her pregnancy period will be passed on easily to her fetus. As explained before, we have seen scientific proof that even HIV+ parents can give birth to normal babies, if proper treatment is given to the fetus itself.

This is not a miracle!

Even though genes play a vital role in transferring the characters of parents to the baby, the negative characters can be overcome by feeding only positive thoughts to the fetus by its mother. This is sure guarantee that the baby born will be a wonderful person in this society. Such is the impact of imprints, thoughts and actions of the expectant mother.

*****

16

MONTH BASED PREGNANT THERAPIES

Do you know Valai kappu, a ritual being done in Tamilnadu situated in south India?

(Valai means "a bangle" and kappu means "to protect" in Tamil Language). This celebration is held by the women of all religions, Hindu, Muslim and Christian, in Tamilnadu.

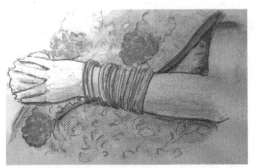

During seventh month, the 'Valaikaapu' function is done to the expectant mother.

The parents and relatives, after worshipping the God, will put bangles made of glass, silver and gold in the hands of the expectant mother. This is to bless the pregnant woman, celebrate her fertility and ensure a safe birth. Also it is believed that the sound of bangles will induce the child's senses.

After that function, she returns and stays at her mother's house for the final weeks of pregnancy.

During this period the expectant mother spends her time reading spiritual books thereby enlightening her spiritual knowledge. After birth, even though the child does not indulge in rituals or spiritual activities, research has proved that the grown up has very high SQ levels.

We have many testimonials which reveal that when we stimulate the neurons at every stage, the born baby will be physically, emotionally and spiritually healthy.

All that the expectant mother has to do is to concentrate on spiritual emotions in this period.

Even though, it can be done by her, she can also get the assistance from the experts in that field. At Dhyanbaby foundation, we have such programmes to enhance her spirituality.

That spiritual programme should be taken in that particular month, i.e., in seventh month.

Undertaking such programme in some other months is not useful. We call it as "month based therapy" programmes.

In the next chapter let us discuss about this "month based therapy" programme elaborately.

*****

17

Meanings of month based Pregnant Therapies

Fifth Month Therapy

In the fifth month, the first important parts of our inner body get accelerated growth.

Even though from the inception of conception, the embryo has got sufficient energy for the growth of all the parts, the five important parts like kidney, liver, lungs, spleen and heart are formed rapidly in the fifth month period.

"Face is the index of our mind" is a dictum. Actually the face shows not only "what is inside our mind", but also "what is ailing us". Such is the wonderfulness of the nature.

It is quite possible for us to find a person who is affected by jaundice by seeing his eyes, is not it? Interestingly, if you compare the shape of the eye it will resemble with that of the liver.

All over the world, there are many kinds of medical practices which can find the nature of internal disease just by analyzing outside organs.

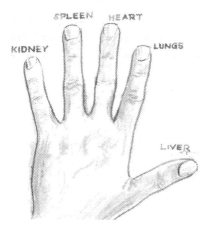

In chakra and Mudra system each of our fingers represents kidney, liver, lungs, heart and spleen. It is shown in the adjacent picture.

Now, let us look into this deeply.

Kidney

You are closing all your fingers except the little finger, what gesture are you making?

Can't you recall now?

Just rewind your memory and go back to your child hood period in which you showed like this to your teacher asking his permission.

For what?

Yes, you asked his permission to go for one toilet (urinating).

(Gestures are culture- specific and can convey different meanings in different social and cultural settings. The gesture described above is used in southern part of India.)

Just imagine! You never showed 'thumb' or other fingers to represent 'Urine'.

Actually the little finger and urinary parts including kidney are related. In "Mudra" and in Chinese ancient medical systems, the little finger represents water element.

Those who have got less water energy, have unhealthy urinary parts.

It is quite natural to get the advice of drinking more water when you approach a doctor for your urinary problem.

Also when you consult with your family astrologer to alleviate some problem, he would probably request you to have a holy bath in the river Ganges or Seas of Rameshwaram or other holy places. You may ask, "Why don't we take such a bath in our house itself!" However, you will get more water energy when you take bath in huge mass of water body.

In our home, if our child cries for no reason in midnight, what we'll do?

We'll bring the child to a temple, where holy water will be sprinkled by the priest on the face of the child. After that the child would sleep well.

What is the secret in it?

Generally, the emotion of fear is reflected in the kidney. According to psychotherapy, shaking off the fear is indirectly done by rocking our bodies. We cannot ask the child to do like that. So, sprinkling water makes the child's body to tingle which automatically shakes off the fear.

Really we have to be thankful to our ancestors who have devised some methods scientifically and spiritually to help us. Anyhow, now we have seen that for the good health of kidney we need water- energy. If there is a shortage of energy in the kidney, these people will be always in fear and have less immunity power. With more kidney-energy, the people will be very strong with self- consciousness and self – discipline without fear.

Spleen

Now, let us come to 'Ring finger'. Even though we wear rings in all the fingers, why this derivative name for this finger only?

Now, think!

In what material is the ring made up of?

Some metal! Right?

Metals are said to absorb cosmic energy and among all metals, gold is said to be having the highest absorption power. As ring finger represents love, wearing metals in this finger will enhance it.

If we have energy of earth, we will have healthy spleen. That is why we wear rings (obtained from earth) in the ring fingers which represent spleen.

Why, in marriage, rings are exchanged and worn in the ring fingers by the couples?

This is because our reproductive system is believed to be controlled by spleen (in Chakra energy system). That is why, to have good children, the couple wear rings in their ring fingers.

With healthy spleen, we will be having good observation power, quick decision making capacity, healthy mind, etc., It helps in producing red blood cells also.

The unhealthy spleen gives us more worry, the habit of eating more and finally ending up with diabetes.

Heart

Now, let us see 'middle finger'. What is the special with this finger? It is longer than other fingers. In other words, we can say it is the tallest among all the fingers, if we keep all the fingers vertically.

What does the "tall" implies?

Suppose, let us consider our TV. We cannot get pictures and sound unless the antenna which is kept on the building is connected to TV. So, to absorb the waves of picture & sound the antenna has to be kept at higher place. The strength of absorption of signals depends upon the height at which the antenna is kept.

In the temples, you might have seen huge tower over the statues of Gods. This is to get the cosmic energy. The height is related to the Universe, the cosmos. The middle finger gets energy from the Universe and gives to the heart. The fire is the element of energy. The heart will be strong and healthy if it gets sufficient cosmic energy. This heart along with thymus keeps the person healthy.

The Thymus is most active from the birth to the age of twelve (adolescent) of a person. That is why in ancient days, in order to get more cosmic energy, our ancestors conducted "Gurukul" studies under the tree.

When the heart is strong, the person will be very kind, and lead a true life. For love & kindness we use the symbol (♥) which is nothing but the shape of heart. If somebody lies, we used to ask him repeating the words again by touching the chest with his hands, where the heart is located. We never ask them to touch ear, or eyes or other parts. So the pure & healthy heart implies true character, noble and straight forwardness.

If this energy is less, that person will not have self confidence and will be a great liar & be always angry with others.

Lungs

It is represented by our index finger. The energy for the lungs is derived from the air. If it gets good energy, the lungs will be in good health and vice versa. Due to ill health of lungs, the person will have the character of finding fault with others.

It can be compared with the gestures we make by showing our index finger towards others and saying," You are guilty!" or "You are wrong!"

But, remember, with the same index finger, with our high energy level, we used to say commanding and encouraging words like "you can do, rise!" "You do like this" etc.

Also we put our index finger on our fore-head when we are deeply thinking.

The persons with healthy 'Lungs,' will have the great administration power, and motivate others with their higher level of thoughts. They, with such high Lung's energy, will become great scientists & eminent personalities.

Our Gandhiji is one of such persons who had achieved great things with this energy. Even though there was no media and many news papers during his period, Gandhiji, sitting in a remote corner of Gujarat, could be able to dissipate his thoughts of freedom to all people from Kashmir to Kanyakumari through simple movement of his index finger. That was his strength!

Another example for the use of this type of energy can be quoted from our Idhikas. Sri Anjaneya is one of the greatest examples.

He is the devotee of Lord Rama. Even then, He could be able to cross over the sea to Srilanka which Rama himself could not do. Once during the war, to save Rama, He brought the hill 'Himalaya' on his palms. How could he do that? That was possible as he was the son of "Vayu" baghavan.

"Vayu" means "air" and "Baghavan "means God. He got all his power through air. That is why He is the great Sage & Prophet.

Liver

Now, we are coming to our thumb. It represents liver. He, who has got sun light and heat energies, will be having strong liver and vice versa. The great achievers used to show their thumps up to imply their "victory".

The liver is responsible for our body beauty, strength, intelligence and prophecy. Scientifically, it is the number one chemical plant in the world. It does more than five hundred types of work. The person who is having less liver-energy has no option than showing their thumps down. They will be adamant, of jealous and relentless.

Let us take care of the liver to become a great achiever.

HENCE, IN THE FIFTH MONTH, IT IS IMPERATIVE TO THE EXPECTANT MOTHERS TO DO SOME MENTAL EXERCISES TO INDUCE THE ABOVE ORGANS OF THE CHILD.

Mental exercises are nothing but positive affirmations which are carefully made. With these affirmations, the expectant mother would speak to the fetus as if it clearly understands her. This kind of mental practice, when done with full belief, will certainly enhance the growth of the above organs.

*****

Sixth Month Therapy

(I.Q. Therapy)

The sixth month is the best time in the overall period of pregnancy to stimulate the IQ cells.

We already knew that the IQ is nothing but the connection between neurons and mainly develops through all the sensory inputs, like hearing, seeing, etc.

Everybody has five senses!

However the individual's perception differs according to the efficient use of those five senses in the world during our learning process.

Actually we are not perfectly "learning" everything!

"Sensory preferences influence the ways in which students learn... Perceptual preferences affect more than 70 percent of school-age youngsters" (Dunn, Beaudry, & Klavas, 1989, p. 52).

"Learning to learn" is a new kind of art.

In general, the children can be of three kinds when comes to learning.

They are 1. Visual, 2. Auditory and 3. Kinesthetic (Tactile).

The 'visual' – type children, learn through pictures. If we say, 'cow' to them, they can immediately picturize the cow in their minds (provided they should have seen the cow). The 'Auditory' –type children will recall the sound, 'ma'. The "kinesthetic' (tactile) – type child, would ask us "This is only picture! Where is the cow?"

The 'tactile' – type would like to understand anything through 'touch-feeling".

Normally, children will show dominance in any one of the above three types. However, in today's world, we need to have at least two of above three types, in order to understand the world and to have correct perception. In order to excel in all the three types of learning, it is recommended to start exercise from mother's womb.

Sense of "smell"

You may wonder about the link between the Intelligence and the feelings received through sensory organs. It is a fact that the persons, who have got strong control over their 'Olfactory' sensor, are showing high degree of intelligence. This "olfactory – sense – development programme" can be given to the child in the womb as well as to the child after the birth & up to the age of 3½.

In our pre-kg school conducted by our foundation, there are also some kids who have taken 'Dhyan baby' programme. When we do one of the exercises for the children, to test their olfactory ability, by asking them to identify the materials which are hidden inside a cloth, the "Dhyan baby" – students would always out do other normal students in smelling the things off.

'Foods for our body',

(Sense of "touch")

We need two kinds of food for our growth. One is for physical and other is for mental growth. For physical growth we need good nutritional food. For mental development, the food is "touch". For all the stages of our life (from fetus to adult), we need the food of "touch".

In human life, the fastest growth happens in the mothers' womb. A dot like embryo becomes three kg of fetus within ten months. All through this period, the fetus is surrounded by a liquid which gives a gentle touch. So the fetus is used to have hundred percent food of "touch" from its mother.

That is why, even after the birth, the child always will be looking for "touch". You may notice that the crying child can be calmed by simply taking him in our hands and hugging him. It is said that the child receives 30% of "touch" up to the age of one. The cradle made of cloth hummock gives such kind of touch.

The expectation for the "touch "will be 60% up to three years old and 50% at the age of five and 30% at seven.

After that, the "Touch" expectation continues constantly with peer group.

So, it is important for the parents to understand this expectation of the child and give sufficient "touch" whenever the child needs it.

For example, if we have sufficient food three times a day, we will not be longing for food. In other case, if we don't take food for a quite some days& if somebody offers us food, we won't check the food for its quality, but we will eat it immediately.

Like this, the child who receives insufficient "touch" will store this deficiency and when it attains "teenage" period, with hormonal changes, it will be ready to receive the "touch" from anybody irrespective of "good" or "bad".

Hence, it is important to stimulate "touch" sense & to give him a virtuous conduct.

Sense of "Taste"

Even though the gustatory senses are spread all over our mouth, they are focused in certain areas of "U" shaped tongue.

When we eat different tastes of food, the relevant glands in our brain are activated. So, we need all the six tastes to activate all the glands.

The children, who have taken the therapy, not only identify the type of material by taste, but also relate the material to some other one. For example, if there is a turmeric powder inside the cloth, they would say, after smelling, "This smell is like the one in the bath room and we use it on our bodies". Other normal children would be able to give answers only after receiving some more clues from us.

 If the children in the age group between 13 and 15 could not differentiate the smell & identify the name of the material, then we may conclude that they have some I.Q. deficiencies. Hence, from this, we may understand the importance of olfactory sense.

In the sixth month therapy, the stimulation of all the senses is done through the power of mental concentration of the expectant mother. That is why this therapy is called IQ therapy. The adjacent picture shows one of such programmes.

Both mother and father are engaged in this therapy and are asked to repeat some positive affirmations. At the background a therapeutic music will be played. With such surrounding, the mother can connect herself with the fetus deeply. Repeating the affirmations four to five times per month is enough to stimulate the baby's senses positively.

*****

Seventh Month

There is a special place of importance for seventh month during the pregnancy period.

Even though the pregnancy itself is a special event for the mankind, irrespective of religions, races, and languages, all people celebrate this "seventh month".

Everybody prays for the child during this month by celebrating it as "Valaikappu" in Tamilnadu, "Seemantham" in Kerala and "Baby Shower" in foreign countries.

The child receives more sensual feeling of mother's mind in this month when compared to other months. If the mother has the "fear" (for some reason) during this month, the child will be born with the attitude of fear.

So, in order to have child with strong mind, the mother has to be happy and courageous.

Also, she has to see many human faces. Suppose, during this period, if she frequently sees & socializes with the family members who are taller than her, the child, after birth will tend to socialize well with taller people. If the child happens to see shorter persons, he will hide himself behind the mother.

This is so because this short stature is not familiar to the child when it was in its mother's womb.

That is why our ancestors have devised some meaningful rituals & formalities systematically for this month.

In the seventh month, after all the rituals of Valaikappu, the expectant mother returns back to her mother's house.

The benefits of valaikappu and returning back to her birth place are,

1) As her mind is fully occupied with the preparation works for going to her mother's house (like taking necessary things for her & her future baby), she won't have time to think about other unnecessary things.

2) In ancient time, no comfortable transport system was available. The pregnant woman had to walk or ride on some uncomfortable vehicle. This gives her extra courage along with the happiness of seeing her mother again. This courageous mind will be helpful to the child.

3) Also during the celebration of "Valaikappu", she becomes well familiar with different kind of people like her friends and relatives (with different heights, skin color, faces etc) and it is recorded in the minds of the child also. So after birth the child will socialize well with all kinds of people.

In ancient time, we were confined to a particular state or country. But, today's lifestyle demands us to go for anywhere in the world. In order to socialize well with those foreigners, is it possible to call all of them to the function of "Valaikappu"?

Not possible!

But, we can bring into our mind all the faces through some special exercise.

Also, in the seventh month, the child starts to dream for the first time. The dreaming cells will be so vibrant and energetic this time. This can be made beneficial by instilling the mother's thoughts into the minds of child. The "seventh month therapy" helps to do this.

Here also very carefully selected affirmations and visualization are important.

By this we can have children of great attitude.

*****

Eighth Month

The eighth month is also very important during the pregnant period.

Normally during the whole pregnant period, it is usual for the expectant mother to have psychological changes. These changes are called "Mood swings".

This mood swing will be said to be at its highest level during eighth month. Physically the child matures during eight month. That is why even if a child is born in miscarriage, it can be saved with latest medical technology and aids. During this period, the rational & logical thinking form.

There is some explanation about this period in vedic culture as below.

"In this time-period in which the logical & rational thinking of the child grows, the child would tend to worry and would be longing to return back to the Universe from where it descended as an atom and grew as a fetus in the mothers' womb. That is why the fetus keeps silence in this period. This 'silence' & 'taking rest' of the fetus is reflected on mother's psychological status".

It is also said that this period is highly suitable to develop S.Q (Spiritual & Social Quotient). This S.Q. will help the child to have the capacity in future to take perfect decision by analysing everything deeply and accurately.

Generally, the children born with induced S.Q. are fortunate ones.

For example, consider the below situation.

One of two children in a house, while playing, touches a burning candle and cries out of pain. The other child just watches this incidence and learns the consequence of touching fire.

Who is smart?

But, actually, if we look into this deeply, we may notice that the other boy has the capacity to learn things through other's experience also. If we want to learn everything only through our personal experience, our life will not be enough to explore the world.

However, those children who have received S.Q. stimulation learn everything in the world not only from their experiences but also from others accurately. They will attain their goals of life completely and easily with clear thoughts.

Do you believe that we can stimulate the spiritual quotient through some magical orisons (magical prayers)?

In the "Microsoft" company in America, a research was conducted with the employees of having same level of I.Q.

Among them, some people were found having higher E.Q which provides those characters like tactfulness, control over their emotions, flexibility and clarity.

Further study revealed some surprising results!

Out of all, only thirty three persons had S.Q. (Spiritual Quotient) in higher levels.

Another point to be noted is out of thirty three people, eleven were Indians.

The secret for having higher level of S.Q was further found as due to magical Orisons that they had especially from the conception period

Further, to find the truthfulness of this secret, the Coco Cola, America, conducted another sort of studies.

In that study, people were equally divided into three groups. First group was asked to do nothing. The second one was asked to repeat the word (chanting) "Coco cola" frequently. The third group was requested to chant their desired Mantras like 'Rama', Krishna, etc. When analysing all the three groups after certain period of time, they finally concluded that the third group had high I.Q, E.Q and S.Q., when second group had medium level in all quotients and the first group hit the bottom in all quotients.

Hence, during this eighth month period, if a mother chants such magical 'mantras' or hears them, it will be beneficial to the child as explained above.

She can also take therapies which taught specific "mantra" suitable for this month.

*****

Ninth Month

From the period of conception to ninth month, the fetus understands the momentary and present time only. From the ninth month, for the first time, it is believed to be thinking of its future.

With only few days left for the birth, in Vedas, the child is said to think about its birth & its future.

A mother cannot request the child to remain in the womb for few more days as she enjoyed the kind treatments during her pregnancy period.

Nor, the child would request his / her mother to keep it in the womb for another one or two month as it would be so comfortable for the child being in the womb.

Both, the mother & child, have to be ready for the birth irrespective of their personal willingness.

Let us consider the following example.

What do you feel if your boss calls on you and gives a deputation letter wherein you are requested to go to the branch in abroad which you don't like at all because of fear about new place, new people, etc...?

Even though that proposal carries a hike in salary and elevation in the job title, you may feel as if to resign the job because of the fear & the feeling of insecurity.

Instead, supposing, if your boss shows you a video clipping using LCD projector and explains,

"Now, you see! You are proceeding from this airport and landing on that airport. A person will be there just outside the airport, waiting for you to take care of you in all aspects. Your new branch office there in that city occupies two hundred Acre of land. See, the video! How big our company is!! In that company, there are two hundred Indian families working for us. You will be having Indian school, Indian restaurant, Indian Hospital, and Indian mall inside the campus itself. So, you will feel the new place as if it is your home town with much safety and security. Moreover, you will be getting additional 5,000 dollar as a salary...." then what will be your reaction?

Won't you readily accept this new offer?

So, there is a difference in going to a place with and without fear, isn't so?

In the same way, it will be a wonderful experience for the mother & child, if they are well prepared during ninth month of pregnancy for natural and comfortable "delivery" which will happen any time after this month.

Hence, it is our duty to prepare the child in the womb to think that it will get the same sort of security and love in the outside world throughout its life same as in the womb.

This month therapy with some special background music provides the mother and the baby with such kind of safety and security.

*****

Tenth Month

While preparing both the mother & baby for the 'delivery', it is equally important to prepare them for "normal delivery".

Our mankind is also belonging to mammals, a class of animals that give birth to live babies and feed them on milk from the breast. The 'normal delivery' is common for all animals.

So only in the time of emergency, to save mother & the child, we should seek "caesarian". Otherwise, we should always try to obtain "Normal delivery".

During normal delivery, if labor starts naturally, then you know that your child is ready to be born. Now, baby's lungs and other major developments have finished maturing and he/she can be able to survive without any medical interventions.

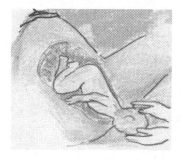

When your baby passes through mother's vaginal opening, the pressure helps to expel the amniotic fluid in the baby's lungs, thus helping to clear away any blockages in the lungs and nasal areas naturally.

Moreover, as the baby passes through vaginal openings and progressively picks up the light, sound and air of the outside world slowly, its consciousness of "coming out to the world "is induced.

Now a day the "normal delivery" is recommended by the doctors all over the world.

To attain this desired goal of normal delivery, some affirmations and visualization techniques can be learnt by the expectant mother either by herself or through some assistance of experts. The affirmations should be words and phrases that are stated in a clear and concise way with a positive emphasis.

Whenever you affirm, feel as though you are drawing the words inside you and as though you are teaching yourself a firm belief. The affirmations like that you are having a normal delivery should be in present tense. You should focus on them as if they are a reality now. You may positively affirm them as often as possible throughout this month.

*****

18

First Year Period

CARE AFTER BIRTH AND MILE STONES TO BE ACHIEVED.

We have shaped up the child all through the pregnancy period by giving appropriate love, health and good notions.

Our hard effort does not end here.

We cannot get melodious music from a veena, a musical instrument, just by making or producing it perfectly. It needs to be fine tuned by giving appropriate twists to the strings, to get perfect "swaram" (note).

Like that, our job is not ending with giving birth to a good baby. The baby needs our help for at least one year from its birth.

Interestingly, all other animals, except human being, would adapt to normal life within few days from their birth. They would start to walk, raise their voices, and start to work as usual within few days. But, human needs at least one year from his birth to speak. The deeds what he learns & does in the first year after his birth differentiate from other animals. This would help him to develop sixth sense.

From the first day of its birth, the baby's all the movements are recorded in its brain.

Each of its movement plays important role in the growth of its knowledge and intelligence.

For example, in our childhood we would have trained in cycling. After that, we would not have the chance to do cycling and would have forgotten.

However, suddenly, for emergency, if we happened to drive bicycle, for our surprise, we'll do it spontaneously. It is because of the recording happened in our brain during the childhood.

So, when we help the child to attain the following seven goals (mile stones) before its first birthday, it will ensure that he can attain maturity physically and mentally and become a successful person. For the mother it is the completion of a **SUCCESSFUL MOTHEHOOD**.

1)SMILING:

From the birth of the baby, it is quite natural for us to expect the baby to recognize and smile. We might have tried many funny ways for the first two months but would have ended with vain. Don't lose your heart. The milestone lies in the end of second month. At this time the sound of your voice is enough to make your baby smile. However, you may try silly faces, tickling peek-a –boo to make the baby smile. That smile will indicate that the baby has achieved its first mile stone.

2) SLEEPING ALL THROUGH THE NIGHT

If the baby starts to sleep all through night and is not disturbing your sleep, it is another mile stone. That means the baby has started to align its bio clock with that of natural clock. This mile stone comes around fifth month (plus or minus one month).

3) SITTING UP

This happens around fifth or sixth month. After straightening and balancing the head, most babies can sit up with the support of resting on their own hands. We may also assist them by providing some small supporting bolsters and pillows. Sitting alone will happen during around eighth month.

4) ROLLING AND CRAWLING

Next comes the mobility. In order to explore the thing around him, the baby needs this mobility.

It starts from just rolling around and then crawling.

Generally, when the child is sleeping, it is not advisable to use pillow or other things around the child as a safety. It will hinder its spontaneous movements like kicking its legs and swinging its arms. Our presence & intervention is necessary only when the child is about to fall off. Other than this, we shouldn't interfere with its free movements.

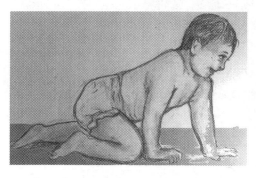

When we allow the child to roll on his own, this continuous rolling motion will be recorded in his mind, and as such in future he can be able to speak without any hesitation and can write continuous letters (i.e., cursive writing). His both sides of the brain will get strengthened when it crawls using its both hands and knees.

This is the mile stone belonging to around eighth month. Some babies may skip this mile stone. However, psychologists recommend that a baby need to complete this kind of activities like rolling, creeping, wiggling and crawling.

So, we may induce the baby to crawl or creep by placing some toys in front of him. Or we may do the act of crawling in front of the baby. Also we may place our hands on his feet, to facilitate him to push himself off for easy crawling.

5) Eating normal food what the family consumes

Mother's milk is enough to the child for the first five months, Milk is primary source of nutrition for new born before they are able to eat and digest other foods. The protein rich &

highly nutrient mother's milk will become Elixir with mother's love and affection, and it is enough for the child for up to six months.

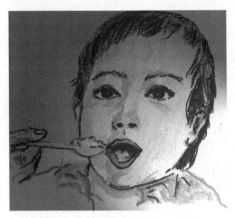

From sixth month, slowly the child can be fed with fruit juice, soups, and porridges, up to eighth month. In Ninth & Tenth months eating of solid foods may be started and whatever we eat may be introduced. In south India, the solid foods are Idlies, Dosas, Chappatti, Idiappam etc. If we follow non-veg, it can also be introduced. The amount of food is not important. The child should taste at least some morsel of all the foods with different tastes.

The amount can be progressively increased in the coming days.

One important thing is that whatever may be the food, the mother's milk should also be mixed along with it at least in small amounts.

As per Indian Vedas and puranas, there existed serpent women, called nagas. They were poisonous to others, but they were healthy by themselves. When they were born as normal human beings, their mother would feed them milk along with very small amount of snake's poison. When mixed with mother's milk, even the poison is digestible for the children.

It can be compared with the difference in our mentality in hospitality that we give to an unknown person when he comes alone and along with another known friend. Naturally we will extend same kind of hospitality as that for our friend to the unknown also.

Hence, the new foods when fed along with accustomed mother's milk, child's body starts to accept.

If the child is trained to use its digestive system to accept all types of food within one year of its age, it will have good food habit and live healthily, throughout its life.

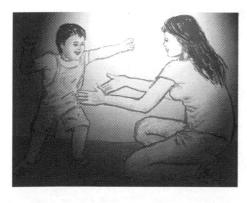

6) STANDING AND WALKING

During eighth month the child will try to stand by holding on to furniture or wall. The next attempt is to take first step.

Who wouldn't enjoy and appreciate the first step taken by the baby?

It will be an unforgettable moment for the parents.

If we want the child to walk in the eighth month, then we have to give training to the child right from the fourth month by allowing him to kick with his legs on our stomach and chest. This would help him to strengthen his legs and enable him to walk in the eighth month. However, the baby, if left unattended, would take its first step during tenth or eleventh month.

We may also provide him some aids like walker to enhance walking ability. It will be well and good if the baby gets such assistance from the hands of father or mother.

7) SPEAKING ATLEAST TWO WORDS

When our goal is to make the child to speak small sentences within his first birthday, his hearing knowledge should be enhanced with frequent and continuous talking with him for, may be, from 2 1/2 months. We may narrate many stories in whatever the language.

Don't think whether the child can understand the meaning. Our brain is amazing that it can be able absorb & learn even up to 14 languages within 3 years of age.

The child would try to imitate the movements of our lips & sounds from our mouth, while we speak to him. Hence, quickly he will learn, within one year, to speak small sentences like, "Mother come!" "Need father", etc. if the child attain this goal, it will be excellent for his skilful speech, in future.

*****

Note: for further details kindly visit www.dhyanbaby.com

19

SHORT STORIES

(Understanding human life from a child's angle)

Foreword:

It is very difficult to answer some of the questions asked by the children. Many times we may wonder about their curious mentality and inquisitive minds. The following stories are the result of interaction had with the moms whose sons underwent Dhyanbaby program.

With some imaginary characters and situations we are trying to answer some delicate (and naughty) questions that present day children may ask us.

(Note: The characters & events in these stories in these stories are only imaginary ones)

Hope you will enjoy reading them!

AUTHORS

19-1

MORAL CODE

"**M**a! Is it a world record, if we do or invent something which is not useful to the man kind?"

Ms. Kavitha fumbled with words to answer his son Krithik, who asked the above question.

For a second, Kavitha could not understand in what angle her son was putting up this question.

"Why son! Why are you asking like that?"

- With this question she attempted to find some time to think about.

"No, ma! I was told that a man has entered in the book of "world records" by inventing a huge pen. Can anybody use that pen, ma?"

Ms. Kavitha could not be able to answer for this question. Instead she tried to distract him. "Go and study your lessons, Krithik! Don't ask such silly questions", she replied.

"All the mums are like that only" Krithik left that place murmuring.

Now, let us analyze the question and try to answer Krithik.

Actually, there exist many answers for this.

The positive answers are,

"The world record is done to show the world the ultimate potential of mankind".

Or,

"To motivate people by doing something that had been considered impossible so far".

On the other hand, the negative answers are,

"Yes, it is a waste of time! He could have done something productive"

Or,

"He is misguiding to do unnecessary things"

Or,

"He is seducing people to do a world record at any cost!"

Which answer is right and which is wrong?

Choosing correct answer depends upon different perceptions of an individual.

Actually, many times, we are at stake, when confronted with such question.

Morality and ethics pose such type of questions.

Yet, the common man still believes that he understands morality. Even those people who think they are very ethical are actually deceiving themselves, because no one can truly know what real ethical is. Thus they cannot be possibly ethical, at least in every one's opinions.

As long as people continue justifying their morals on differing standards (religious, non-religious, societal norms, etc) there will always be conflict and strife. And where strife exists, humanity's problem will also exist.

There is not a single line that splits up ethics and un- ethics perfectly. Somebody draws a line close to "ethics" and still being in the un-ethical area, work on some principles and evade their true identities.

However, one thing is certain!

If good morals and ethics are well planted in the minds, there will be no more confusion.

The confusion and conflicts starts when somebody who has got immoral code in his mind attempts to act with moral characters which he has recently studied through some books or advices.

Can you be sure that you teach all the ethics that you have learnt, to your children?

How many times, have we wondered on seeing the ethical characters with our children, which even we have not taught to them?

From where did the ethics come?

Like intelligence, the ethics have also been evolved over a period of time and not invented by human kind at one period of time. We can logically conclude that as mankind developed higher intelligence, the concept of morality and ethics became better developed in the human psyche too.

And that too, the strong implantation of such ethical knowledge to successive human kind entirely depends on mothers. Mind it, with the exception of the fetus, who can actually do the miracle of sitting silently in a private room and learning things attentively for the whole period of at least six months!!

*****

19-2

TO STRIKE THE BALANCE

"**H**ereafter you have to be very careful Padma! Take as much rest as possible. Don't move yourself suddenly!", Kavitha was advising her friend Padma over phone, who is pregnant, when Krithik, her son interfered her conversation.

"Ma! Won't anybody be there to give such advices to the pregnant cat that we saw the other day? How to stop the cat hitting the wall and hurting her baby inside her belly?" he was wondering.

Two days before, Krithik was showing her the cat which was jumping here and there over the wall and exclaimed why its belly was too big. Kavitha had explained him that the cat was pregnant. Then, Krithik, expressing his worry, asked his mother, "won't it hurt the baby cat when the mother cat hit the wall, ma?".

Kavitha had calmed her son by saying that it was natural.

Now, again, as usual, she was speechless when Krithik asked the question. Even though, Krithik raised this question out of innocence (or may be, he was, "naughty"), one thing is clear to us that we have started looking pregnant women as a "patient" instead of a person being in a state of holy motherhood.

Motherhood has to be enjoyed and not to be feared. It doesn't mean that you have to enjoy by jumping with joy like that cat. We have to strike the balance naturally.

Balance is central to the universe. Actually, the man's spirit too seeks to balance life with the right amount of everything, in order to feel worthy and fulfilled.

"To strike the balance" is otherwise called "moderation". In our own dictionary, we have unfortunately removed the word "moderation". Moderation can be applied to all parts and walks of life.

We could see the people who are in pursuit of reducing their body weights, forgetting about "moderation" and listening to different and contradictory advices by dieticians, end up in becoming "alien like-creatures".

We could also see some people who don't have the ability to strike the balance between life and work, end up in hospitals as patients. It is worrying to notice that the incidence of Repetitive Stress Injuries (RSI) has shot up during the past decade, owing to mental conflict arising from a lack of work-life balances.

We have seen people who could not even think of having emotions in week days and reserve emotions for the week-ends. They are boasting of calling themselves as workaholics.

Through "moderation", they can realize that there is more to life 'than working for a livelihood and acquiring assets. We can write volumes on moderation. In the context of pregnancy, there is no ideal "moderation" which can be applied to all. It is a dynamic concept, which differs for each individual. Our job is to let the woman understand and enjoy her pregnancy and take care of herself in her moderate ways.

*****

19-3

DESIRE OR SATISFACTION-
WHICH IS RULING US?

"Can't we live without onion for some time, ma?"

As usual the innocent Krithik's question made his mother Kavitha to become tightlipped.

She could understand that the naughty boy was raising this kind of doubt when she was exclaiming and complaining about the sky- rocketing prices of onion to her friend over phone. She had been complaining about the inefficiencies of authorities concerned in curbing onion prices.

However, his question opened her up new vistas of answers. Her mind started to explore her pool of knowledge for possible answers.

She could bring back to her memory about the people whom she knew already and who live very happily without using onion for so long time. Even though they avoid onion due to the restriction laid by the religion, actually, health wise they did not lose anything.

"When they could live for a long time devoid of onion, why can't we live for a short period of time?" she thought.

She slowly started to realize that Lord is not such a miser to leave all His own creatures to die starving for food.

Now, let us analyze.

There is more than enough of "abundance" around us that are created by Lord for us. We, just, are showing our ignorance by not feeling or finding them!

If we can't afford onion, why don't we take other equally nourished and cheaper varieties? Why do we all fall on the same thing and create an artificial demand for the perishable thing? If we wait for another two days with our hands crossed, the prices will automatically come down! But, why are we not doing like this?

So the whole drama was created by us, but we complain others for not exercising his authorities which are beyond their control.

If we start to look for the other best alternatives that the Lord has provided for us, there will not be any speculation. With speculation we pay more than what the particular thing really deserves.

"Why this subject, now?" you may ask.

It has been found that, the parts of brain responsible for "desire" and "satisfaction" are in different areas, with the "desire" part always stronger than that of the other. That is why dissatisfaction will result even if we cater to the full needs of "desire" part.

On one hand, such type of dissatisfaction leads to positive result in which we always thrive for new things and find new better things for better life standards. On the other hand, if we leave it unchecked, it will lead us to disaster.

Persons who can balance these two feelings will ultimately win the race.

Again, the controlling power may be strengthened by imbibing such strong thoughts from the womb.

The scripts of balancing acts of expectant mother may be of much helpful to her offspring, in applying the same in later stages.

*****

19-4

PROACTIVENESS

Moments before, he had not realised that he would encounter such an end!

With all sorts of luxuries on his body—branded dresses, branded cooling glass and so on-he was enjoying the cool breeze that was passing on him while he was riding a bike. He had adjusted the rear-view- mirror so as to reflect his face on it. Then and there, he was viewing the mirror and was satisfied himself with what he saw on it.

Some moments later....

Before he could shift his eyes from the mirror, he missed to notice that the bike had arrived at a sharp U-bend.

Despite with the rapid signals from his brains to all his body- motor- mechanism, the reactions were so slow that he had to turn the bike more or less at the same speed.

Soon he lost control, and as the centripetal force was higher than the gripping force exerted by the tyres on the road, the bike started to skid on the road

The next day, he was smiling in the picture in the obituary column of a local news paper.

This is one of many incidences where we show our complete negligence. Unless, otherwise, we are forced by stringent legislations or other strong external forces, we are not even attempting to follow not only safety rules but also some ethical rules.

It may be due to complacency or to satisfy our perverted mind which says 'I'm different from others, and my way is different'.

or is it to show heroism?.

But, whatever may be the root cause which arises out the evil inside us and ultimately brings us to the grave, we may avert this with our continuous learning and practice in our earlier life.

That sort of character is called pro activeness.

The proactive person doesn't need any advice or instructions. Proactive behavior involves acting in advance of a future situation, rather than just reacting. It means taking control and making things happen rather than just adjusting to a situation or waiting for something to happen.

Spoon-fed children always expect directions from his parents or others. Let us help our off springs to become proactive persons. So, let us start teaching him right from the womb.

*****

19-5

DREAM, DREAM, DREAM

That high-pitched sound woke up Ms. Kavitha.

Out of utter tiredness, she had been sleeping deeply. However, the scream was so powerful that she was almost thrown out of bed. It took several seconds for her to bring herself to back her consciousness and to understand that the scream belonged to Krithik, who was sleeping beside her.

She patted him gently and whispered in his ears, "Krithik, everything is O.K., you are alright". Krithik opened his eyes for a moment and then slowly slipped into his deep sleep.

The next day,

Ms. Kavitha was on the phone chatting with her friend.

"Something is haunting here at nights! Krithik, recently, is, screaming on seeing something in his dreams! Should we perform any special pooja (some rituals)?"

In the mean time, her husband was overhearing their conversation.

He started to respond.

"Why are you so conservative Kavitha? You need not worry for such kind of trivial things."

Putting off the phone she said," You would not be advising like this if you had heard his cry. You escaped as you were on tour".

Her husband smiled and asked her the question.

"What are dreams?"

He did not expect answer from his wife. So he continued. "There are many schools of thoughts about dreams. Actually many persons are earning money by acting like interpreters for dreams and by assigning (their own) meanings to dreams".

Stopping his smile, he continued.

"Every night, we shut our eyes, let our mind slip and enter the blank limbo of sleep. While it is tempting to treat sleep simply as a state of unconsciousness, now, we have different story, in which, sleep is really not as far from waking as it first appears. All persons whilst they are awake are in one common world, but, each of them, when is asleep, is in a world of his own".

"When REM sleep was first discovered several decades before, it was thought to be the only sleeps phase in which dreams occurred".

"Sleep researchers have concluded that the brain never actually shuts down at night. Brain cells have no "off" button, and actually, they must fire a few times each second just to stay alive and healthy. When all external sights and sounds are blocked the brain tries to make sense of the random images which we frequently saw or we had been thinking deeply. The bad things that we saw result in bad dreams and vice versa. It is crazy for some people to watch horror movies until mid-night, and then screaming in the sleep for the rest of all the night".

Kavitha's laugh interrupted his speech for a moment.

She asked her husband through the laughs, "Then, how can we have a sound sleep which is very much necessary for repairing our body and mind?".

The husband calmly replied. "It is being said that the process of dreaming starts as early as in our life. The baby starts its dreaming process from the seventh month in the womb. That is why our ancestors give priority for seventh month by doing some special celebrations".

"Normally, we have no conscious influence on our dream imagery - we are passive observers.

But, another type of dream is there which we call as lucid dreaming. In lucid dreaming, people can control their dream experiences. Lucid dreaming is not just entertaining - it can be therapeutic. People can overcome phobias, for example, by confronting and controlling them in lucid dreams"- at one breathe he explained Kavitha about the dream.

Kavitha was happy to be convinced. She let off the notion of doing some rituals as a measure of remedy for Krithik's "Dream-scream".

"As mother's dreams are said to be affecting their off springs, why don't we learn the art of lucid dreaming?"- Author

*****

19-6

GESTATION PERIOD - THE NATURAL LAW

"**K**avitha, you should be patient! Things will automatically change for good"

Kavitha's mother was attempting to console her but Kavitha could not control herself from crying. Her eyes shed copious tears as she leaned on the shoulders of her mother.

"Anyway, my dear daughter! I will come again tomorrow! We will discuss it again in detail".

Saying this, Kavitha's mother left her.

The next day...morning...

Kavitha was preparing tiffin- box for her son Krithik for the noon meal. She cut one mango and put it in one of the tiffin boxes.

When she was about to pack the box, Krithik came in panting.

"Ma! Please give me one slice of mango now, ma".

Kavitha handed over him one slice of mango.

It almost suddenly disappeared into Krithik's mouth.

For one moment, he closed his eyes enjoying the taste of mango.

Then he suddenly asked his mother, "Ma! Isn't it the same mango which was sour last week? and... this week... very sweet?!!!"

Kavitha replied him "Yes, my son! That is the period for ripening!"

"So, if we wait, even the sour will become sweet, won't it, Ma!" Krithik asked.

This question suddenly made the truth to be dawn on her. Yes, now she could understand the meaning of what her mother advised her yesterday. "Always we have to be patient and give time to the things which are not in our control to change on their own".

The realization of truth made the happiness to re- enter into the minds of Kavitha.

It is true that even a farmer knows that he cannot sow and reap on the same day!,

That is the gestation period and natural law! The gestation period actually means the time between the conception and labour. However, we can apply the concept of gestation period for all things in which patience is needed.

We have to understand that each thing has its own gestation period. Nature has given the tiny animals to have the gestation period of about thirty days and for big animals like elephant it is 650 days.

So, we should not be hurry and urge big things to happen immediately. Patience is a sort of good character that everyone should possess. While doing our duty well and with complete dedication, one should keep patience. This will always make us a successful person.

Like that, the expectant mother also should possess patience during pregnancy period. She has to do many things during this period to her baby.-- Author

*****

19-7

REAL SUCCESS OF THE SOCIETY

"**I** am very much pleased to see the talents shown by the students of this school on this great occasion of the Annual day celebration! I especially admire the speeches delivered by the students in English! The laudable......."

The chief guest of that Annual day celebration was so kind enough to make the area inundated with her praising!

Ms Kavitha was little bit worried that her son Krithik did not participate in any one of the programmes.

"You seem to be worrying, Ma?"

Krithik somehow noticed the feeling of her.

Ms Kavitha could no longer control her feeling and in spite of her hard efforts the tear filled her eyes. She pretended as if a dust fell into her eyes.

"Ma, I can understand your feeling" Krithik spoke softly, "You are worrying that I haven't got any prize through participation, aren't you?"

"Yes! Isn't a shame, Krithik?" finally she exploded... but with low voice.

Krithik had already been fed up with the comparisons that her mother always made. So, he, before she starts to tell something, would like to defend himself.

"See, Ma! This is an advertisement of our school to show the world that their students can speak English fluently. But, do you think, are all our students equally well versed with English? I know how much strain that the boy took before appearing on this dais. The praise by the chief guest is really worthy if she could select any one of the students in the auditorium and ask the student to speak in English on any subject." Krithik was seemed as if prating.

"You are justifying your behavior, Krithik!" Kavitha retorted. However, she could understand the truth in his statement. Real success of our society is to make all students as experts.

Even though our education system, she thought, could provide equal opportunities, then how come the difference among students in the ability of learning.

She got the answer in the subsequent week when she attended a discourse in which the Bhisma was said to explain the power of mothers as the panacea of all kinds of calamities. With mothers' strong will power, Bhisma was said to narrate, one could-make an equal and harmonious world. If our mothers follow the vedic rules laid by our ancestors strictly, the youth, the future pillars of our nation, will certainly be still strong.

From that day onwards, she stopped comparing Krithik with other boys and instead concentrated on enhancing his own strengths.

As Sri Chinmayandhaji told, the youth are not careless, they are cared less. The youth are not useless, they are used less.

Let the mothers make our nation great!

*****

19-8

MANAGING RELATIONSHIPS

"**M**a! Whom should we punish, is it the person who did encroach upon the other person's field, or, the person who did allow the other person to enter into his field by not putting proper fence?"

Kavitha felt some chill passing through her spines!

She could not control her feelings which she had kept under tight lid for many years from surfacing. She had bad experiences by allowing other persons to enter into her personal circle and had lost her own identities in fulfilling the expectations of her relatives, friends and had suffered mentally.

'What a weird question, Krithik is asking! What had happened to him?" she thought.

She started worrying inside as this type of question should not have come from a child of ten years old.

'Is my Krithik is in trouble?!" unable to think further, slowly she asked him, "Have you got into unnecessary trouble?"

"No, Ma!" -he smiled at her as usual. She melted away at his charming smile, as usual.

"I was watching the movie 'Ranuva veeran' (*a Tamil movie*). After a heavy fight at the train and sending the thieves off, our hero Rajini would say to the newly married couple that it is not the fault of thieves, but, the fault of us to tempt them to steal our jewels by openly exhibiting them on our bodies. Ma, after that, just I was thinking deeply. And, now, I am asking this question. Actually, I am not in to any trouble, don't worry!"

Kavitha was relieved by his answer. However, she was unable to find the answer for his question.' It may be correct or may not be' she thought.

Finally she managed to reply her son. "Whether it is right or wrong, my son, it is our duty to form a shelter around us and be in safety. There is nothing wrong in it."

But, she was not sure about her answer.

The next day, when she was explaining this event to her friend, the friend giggled. "What you said is correct, Kavitha" She told.

"It is also a natural law and it can be applied in managing our relationship also."

"Would you please explain?" Kavitha requested her friend.

"Well, Kavitha! You might have known about valence of atoms in science."

"Yes.'

"Each atom has a definite number of circles around its centre in which a definite number of electrons are orbiting" The friend continued," if the atom allows additional electron from other atom or lose one electron from it, then, it will

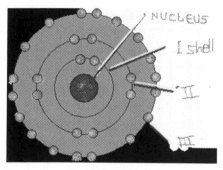

not be stable and will become ions. Moreover you might have noticed that only the electrons in the outer layer move from one atom to another." The friend gasped a moment.

"What are you going to tell?" Kavitha asked.

"It is same like managing our relations. We should have at least three layers around us. The inner most one which is called intimate circle which is for all our close relatives like our father, mother, husband, wife and our children. The second one is for close friends. The third one is for social relationship. Each layer would take only definite numbers only. Mostly depending upon how well we fit our timings to each relationship. The conflict and confusion occur when we allow relationships in the wrong layer. "The friend concluded," Now, I think you might have understood my point."

"Yes, my friend! The nature has readymade answers for us! The only thing is we should prepare ourselves to perceive the truth from it" Kavitha sighed with great satisfaction.

*****

19-9

LEARNING A LESSON FROM THE TREE

"Why the trees are shedding their leaves?" This question must have arisen in your mind when we were walking through our garden and seeing lot of leaves being scattered on the ground.

or

You would have received a request from your servant about increasing his per hour wages because of additional work for him to remove plenty of rubbish of leaves around the garden.

or

You might have worried about the deterioration of appearance of our house because of the lean trees which had shed their leaves!

or

You might have sighed about thinking of the disposal of huge amount of fallen leaves!.

This happens every year! Whether we wonder, complain or whatever do, the trees continue to do their "shedding off leaves- function" during every change of season from summer to winter!.

Yet after the end of winter, the trees again come back alive with still more tender and green leaves!

Why they shed their leaves?

To answer this question, we first have to understand what leaves are and what they do.

Leaves are nature's food factories. Plants take water from the ground through their roots. They take a gas called Carbon-di-oxide from the air. Plants use sunlight to turn water and carbon dioxide into oxygen and glucose.

Oxygen is a gas in the air that we need to breathe. Glucose is a kind of sugar. Plants use glucose as food for energy and as a building block for growing. The way plants turn water and carbon dioxide into oxygen and sugar is called photosynthesis. That means "putting together with light." A chemical called chlorophyll helps make photosynthesis happen. Chlorophyll is what gives plants their green color.

As summer ends and autumn comes, the days get shorter and shorter. This is how the trees "know" to begin getting ready for winter.

During winter, there is not enough light or water for photosynthesis. The trees will rest, and live off the food they stored during the summer. They begin to shut down their food making factories. The green chlorophyll disappears from the leaves. As the bright green fades away, we begin to see yellow and orange colors. Small amounts of these colors have been in the leaves all along. We just can't see them in the summer, because they are covered up by the green chlorophyll. Then leaves start to fall off!

But, during this period, even though the trees are seemed dormant, actually they are happily living using their internally stored energy!

Now, you might have understood what analogy I am going to make by learning this lesson from the nature.

Yes, just be calm whenever trouble comes and don't be entirely dormant at that period and finally when chances are again showing up, sprout like the tree again!

*****

19-10

WHAT IS THE REAL NEED TO OUR CHILDREN?

Even inside the fully air-conditioned hall, Ms Kavitha had to use her hand -towel to wipe off the beads of perspiration standing out on her fore head.

She had been in search of best toy available in the market which was to be presented to the two-year old daughter of her friend as a birth day gift.

When she entered the mall specially meant for kids, she could not leave anything aside!

Even, for her age, every toy was amusing and confusing her about the selection!

That was actually the third mall she was searching for the best toy! She came out of the previous two malls hoping to get still better one in the next mall.

Now she was still in dilemma!" Which one should I select? Will it prove my worthiness in the party?" she was thinking.

However, she had to finalize the purchase immediately, as she had the birth day function in the evening, and, now, already the clock was showing 12:30 PM. She had to rush to make her and her son, Krithik, up for the party. Finally, she, somehow, managed to select one toy!

In the evening, she attended the birth day function along with Krithik.

There was lot of crowd. Every person attending the function was carrying a parcel of gift. Krithik could not control himself in getting envy with the two-year old child when she was inundated with the gifts from everybody.

Finally, when they returned from the party, Krithik asked his mother hesitatingly," Ma! Do you thing the child will have enough time to play with all toys?"

For a moment Kavitha was silent as she could understand the envying tone in Krthik's voice.

However, a strong question rose in her mind.

"Isn't Krithik correct? How come a little child could devote all her time to play with all the toys? Wouldn't the child miss all other entertainments like socialising with her brother and sister and parents?.. and entertaining with other natural things?".

She, then, felt sorry that she spent lot of her time in the selection of the toy and presenting it just for the name- sake, to a baby who, actually, might not have enough time to play with.

Without giving any answer to his son, just she pulled and hugged him. Krithik was happy as if he got the answer.

Actually one of the greatest things about the children is that they have the ability to entertain themselves for a long time with something as simple as a card board box or even a piece of paper!.

It makes you wonder why we feel the need to buy them so many toys that they won't even have time to play with them all before they grow out of them.

Often, if we take the time to question our compulsion of giving our children new toys and clothes, and to spoil them with food that is not even good for them, we will find that we are trying to fill up the space to avoid our own difficult feelings and pain.

If you feel yourself wanting to spoil your child with material possessions, take a moment and see if you can feel where your motivation is coming from.

We may be inundating our children with things they don't need, out of our own desire to create a feeling of abundance that was lacking in our own childhood, or out of a need to feel liked by our children. Both of these motives tend to be unconscious, stemming from unresolved issues from our own upbringing.

These unresolved feelings naturally come up when we find ourselves in the role of a parent, when our child reaches the age we were when these traumas were most pronounced.

Spoiling your children will not save you or make your pains disappear. Only acknowledging and working on your emotional issues can do that. What our children really need us to provide for them is both a sense of safety and a sense of freedom and love. If we are able to do this well, material possessions need not take center stage.

We all want to provide our children with a good and happy life, but most of us know deep down that material possessions play a very small role. We confuse our children when we seek to make them happy through buying them things. When we do this, they take our cue that happiness comes in the form of toys and treats, rather than in the joy of being alive, surrounded by love, and free to explore the world.

So, let our children enjoy the world naturally!

*****

19-11

MIND WASHING!!

The ball whizzed past Krithik's ear. For a moment he stumbled and fell on the mud. His clothes were smeared with mud.

"Oh no! I am again going to face my mom's scolding" Krithik's body shivered with fear when an angry face of his mom appeared in his mind.

He was playing cricket with his friends in the street.

Brushing aside the fear and the giggles of his mocking friends, he continued to play.

However, the second ball batted by his friend was really a challenging one. The ball was so tricky in escaping from his clasps and making a thundering sound when shattering the window glass of the house nearby.

"Oh, my! Now, hundred percent punishment from my mom is confirmed" Krithik thought.

When he looked around to see what other boys were doing, he could not believe his eyes!

Everybody had vanished! He started to return to his house.

The thought process was so powerful!

His mom was waiting for him in the house with furious face, as he thought.

It was sure that she had received a complaint call from the owner of the house whose window was shattered by the ball played by Krithik's team.

Her angry become boundless when she saw Krithik smeared with mud all over his body and clothes.

She almost exploded immediately!

"How many times should I tell you to stay inside the house during your summer holidays? Always behaving mischievously and making you and your clothes so dirty!

Do you think I should always devote all of my time for washing your clothes even in your holidays and replying to the angry neighbor's complaints? Next year, I will ask your father to make you enroll in any one of the residential schools! Then only, you will understand about good manners and about me.."

While Kavitha's mouth was busy in delivering a non-stop discourse for at least for half an hour, her hands gave some slaps on Krithik.

Krithik, not bearing the pain, also finally erupted,

"Stop, ma! The dirt on clothe and body can be washed and cleaned, but, how to cleanse the dirt that you are making in my mind through such scolding!"

The above incidence may seem normal to most of us. However, as Krithik told, the dirt of negativity would creep into our mind and stay there without our permission.

The Children who are actually a weaker section are more susceptible to such poisoning of mind. The poisoning is not only from the parents or mocking friends, but also through recent inundated information technology.

While we are responsible for protecting our children, we also should take care of ourselves to cleanse such negative dirt from our mind as clean mind is always happy and deliver good results.

But, how?

It is so simple!

Just get rid of the unnecessary information that is flowing through many channels for at least one day per week.

For at least once per week, do simple meditations like taking a good sleep, doing simple exercise, simply watching our breaths, listening songs and having simple food containing fruits and vegetable.

And see how they soothe your mind as well as your body!

And how you transform yourselves ensuring not being the part of the reason for the nasty incidence that we described above!.

And rest of the week don't indulge in doing the things that you consider not good for you even though your evil side urges you and requests you to do JUST ONCE.

Let us be happy and make the younger generation happy.

*****

19-12

SPIRITUAL ENLIGHTENMENT

"**W**here do you want to go, Madam?" asked the bus conductor.

With the relief of getting a comfortable seat, Kavitha replied, "Madurai!"

She was going to Madurai along with her son Krithik to Meenakshi Temple.

Whenever she got a mental grief, she used to go to Meenakshi Temple to lodge complaint with God Meenakshi.

Normally the complaint would be against the God Meenakshi herself as to" why She is punishing her always?" or "Are you guiding my life correctly?"

With many thoughts hovering in her mind, Ms. Kavitha kept silence for a long time until Krithik's voice pulled her up from the drowning thoughts.

"Ma! Do you know the way to Madurai?"

With a forced smile on her lips Kavitha replied, "No! my son."

"Then how can it be sure that we reach our destination correctly".

Kavitha was silent thinking for a moment.

Then she replied, "My son! I trust the driver as he knows the way very well".

"Ma! Why don't we check up with the driver then and there whether he is going in the right path?" Krithik asked his mother innocently.

"Son! If everybody starts to ask and disturb the driver, he cannot drive, but stop the bus frequently for answering the questions" The mother replied.

"Isn't the same rule being applied to God who drives all of us, ma?"

The mother could not speak when realizing the truth in his words.

"My son is correct! Why am I frequently visiting Meenakshi temple? Am I checking the God? or creating an impression that I am pious?" she thought.

But, certainly she knew one thing!

She already had an answer for all her sufferings! She continued to think.

"One thing that I have to do is to correct my belief-system in order to get rid of my worries!

That is to believe the God strongly!" Finally she concluded.

Kavitha changed her mind and converted this trip to thank the God for steering her in the right path and not for lodging any complaint or checking the God!

The above story depicts the spiritual quotient which the boy exhibits. So long as we blame outside sources, our miseries will continue and we will feel helpless. All religions have been teaching us about the inward journey to discover the essence of our being, to harness our mind and to channelize all our energy for great performance.

Knowing about the religion and doing some rituals will not yield a good spiritual enlightenment. In our above story Ms. Kavitha knew about the religion. But knowledge was not transferred into wisdom. However, her son had got some spiritual wisdom.

*****

19-13

LIVING SPONTANEOUSLY

Kavitha was astonished with her son's question. She never thought of this in that angle before. How come such an intelligent question out of a small brain? She wondered!

The event began like this.

When Kavitha was in the kitchen, her son Krithik entered the kitchen asking, "Mom! Did the cat visit again to steal the milk?"

Kavitha's eyes showed some sort of triumph.

She replied with a smile, 'No my dear! He did not turn-up last night! I have taught him a lesson!"

"What did you teach him, ma?"

"Simple! As you studied the story of Tenali Rama, I kept very hot milk yesterday. The hot milk has taught him a lesson by writing strong remarks on his tongue! I think, from now on, we can leave the fear of losing our milk every night to these thieves!

Krithik was thinking for a moment and then asked. "Ma! Do you think, there is only one cat around here? How your teaching to one cat will stop other cats from stealing our milk, ma? Will this cat tell other cats about your punishment, ma?"

This might be an intelligent question from a small boy, even though Krithik had raised that question out of his innocence.

The above is actually a story and not a real incident! However, every one of us might have encountered such incidences and have appreciated our kids for their intelligence.

In the above story, when Kavitha had perceived the incidence based on her past experience/data, the boy, Krithik was spontaneously asking the question without any prejudice. He was trying to capture the real fact.

In fact, our quality of life will improve, if we can retain this type of character of that child throughout our live.

That is living spontaneously! Living with agility!

The intelligence is the ability of the brain to process information leading to true conclusion.

To assess the intelligence, the psychologists over a very long period, have designed many tests and the scores derived from the tests are expressed as IG (Intelligent Quotient). The IQ of average person is around 100. There are so many influencing factors that affect IQ level. It starts from maternal (fetal) environment, to family environment, to the genes and the the health.

Can we artificially make intelligence?

Here is the scientific way of improving IQ? (May be a crazy one!)

Suppose we have microchips that exactly behave like brain cells.

Now, we replace one brain cell with that micro chip.

What will happen?

If all the inputs and outputs remained precisely the same, we would never notice the difference.

And what if another, then another cell was replaced, until gradually all 100 billion neurons in our brain had been turned to silicon.

Would there ever come a point where we stopped being us? Would be become an intellectual machine?

These are the questions that scientists have been throwing at each other since the dawn of computer era. Still, science has no answer for that.

The above is just a crazy thinking!

Besides good nutrition, good environments, the script taught by mother to the fetus is also said to be one of the influencing factors for IQ improvement.

If mother forms a strong bond during maternity, it continues to be strong even after birth and this bond results in good family environment for the child to develop still more IQ level.

*****

19-14

WHAT YOU THINK IS WHAT YOU ARE!

"Passengers of flight IQ 517 are requested to go to A-1 gate. The boarding has started."

When Kavitha heard the announcement, she and Krithik are at B-30. They had almost stranded by window-shopping. Being first flight experience for Krithik, he had been so inquisitive in asking many questions about whatever he was seeing in the air-port.

«A long way to go «Kavitha thought.

"We have to rush, Krithik" saying this, she almost dashed dragging Krithik with her. Krithik could not get proper answer for why they were suddenly rushing. But, he was enjoying that too.

They jogged through the port skimming up many escalators, onto a tram back down and around and finally into a waiting room where nobody was there except some air port official and one official almost barking on them.

"Come quickly! It is almost closing time".

Kavitha and Krithik somehow managed to speed up their last paces and boarded into the plane.

Inside the plane, they had to sit in two different places. A richly looking old man was sitting nearby the seat of Krithik.

Then came the announcement for the take –off!

The hostesses showed and instructed the safety practices to be followed inside the flight and during critical time.

Krithik was enjoying every moment with great amusement.

After take-off, when one of the hostesses offered him chocolate, he asked, "madam, what a fortunate person you are! You can fly daily in the plane, can't you?"

With a gentle smile the hostess nodded her head.

"Madam! Did you think in your child hood that you would fly in the plane?" Krithik let a second question.

"It was my dream from my childhood to become a hostess, boy! I focused all my life collecting information about this job and prepared myself" She proudly said.

"Great!" Krithik appreciated her.

Then his attention turned to the old man sitting next to him.

"Sir!, Do you travel by plane frequently?"

"Of course, almost daily" The old man replied.

Krithik could not control his excitement.

"So, sir, did you also think from your child hood that you would fly in air-plane daily."

"No, my boy! I was living in a village where I had the only opportunity to see the planes flying over in the clouds. At that time I thought it was a toy and would like to own it. Then it became a great desire for me. Now, I am the owner of this flight."

Krithik could not stop his lower jaw from dropping out of amazement.

He could realize the power of thought process.

Now, we can have the following three interpretations from the above story.

One is the "power of thought in making the things to happen"

Second---the overwhelming ideas and information about the hostess-job has made the lady to long for being hostess and finally became a hostess.

Third---the old man, who made the decision of owning an airplane out of innocence in his child hood period and did not give up his thought of owning a flight (irrespective of many hurdles and negative information).

So, what you think is what you are!

We are responsible for our thinking. Let us develop and have the power of filtering junk-thoughts and to have good ones which make us great!

*****

19-15

WHAT IS GOD'S LANGUAGE?

Kavitha could not understand what her son Krithik was trying to ask.

It was Vijayadhasami day- A day in which all Hindus worship God Saraswathi, (God for education and knowledge).

"Krithik! Keep your all books in front of Lord Saraswathi! Let us worship her now. Tomorrow, while again doing pooja, you have to read at least one page from each book in front of Lord Saraswathi"

Krithik did all what she asked him to do. Even she could not believe her eyes when he chanted mantras during the worship.

The next day, morning, when they again assembled in the pooja room, Kavitha asked him to read the books.

He was reading one page from each book interestingly.

Then, suddenly he asked the question. "Ma, what is God's language?"

Kavitha could not understand what her son Krithik was trying to ask.

"From where are you getting such questions, Krithik? What is your doubt?" she asked.

"Ma, now, I am reading books of different languages- Tamil,  English and Sanskrit, etc. Can the Lord understand all languages? Like that can he hear and understand the prayers of other French and Japanese people?"

Kavitha thought for a while. "It is very weird question! How can I answer his question?"

"Krithik, come here! I will give you some answer!" His father working in a computer called him.

Krithik came up to his father.

"See, this computer Krithik! Tell me, what language do you observe from the monitor?"

"English" Krithik replied.

"Do you think that the computer CPU could understand the language?"

"Yes of course! Then, how it could bring up the results?"

"The language we are using is different from what it can understand. It only knows binary language which is a sort of 'on'- the presence of electrons and 'off'- the absence of electrons".

Krithik keenly listened to what his father was saying.

"Whatever language we enter through key board and ultimately what appears on the monitor are for our understanding. But, they are converted into binary language and finally the computer does the same job for all types of languages with the same meaning. Now, can you understand, Krithik?"

"Yes, father! Now, I understand! I have heard that the Lord is the sole energy. He understands us through the energy waves that we liberate irrespective of our language. If we liberate positive energy we get positive results and vice versa. Isn't correct?"

The father could see bright light in Krithik's eyes.

"You are right!" Saying this, the father turned towards Kavitha who was still in amusement with his answer.

*****

19-16

5 'S' TO OUR MIND

"Ah! At last I've found it!" Kavitha's eyes expressed her happiness. She sighed with the great relief of finding that article. She had almost made her room topsy-turvy in search of that article for the past several days.

"It's been here only! But I could not see it! Strange! Isn't so?" She wondered herself.

Krithik, watching this, was also wondering "How come these things get out of our sight when we search for them?"

- His young mind immersed in deep thought.

"Ma, why don't they show up in our first attempt of searching? Is there any difference in the quality of our searching?" – He asked his mother.

'Answering some of the questions raised by to-days children is really complicated!' Kavitha understood.

Now, as she was also in the same state, she could not answer his question immediately.

However, her husband came in to her rescue.

"It doesn't depend upon the quality of searching, Krithik. It depends on some simple rules. Even though everybody knows it, they fail to understand this simple thing and implement what they have learnt. If we follow simple rules, we don't need to waste our valuable time in searching for material things".

The husband paused for a brief moment and enjoyed watching the curiosity on both faces of mother and son.

Then he continued explaining about simple rules.

"One of the systems which contains these simple rules can be learnt from Japanese way of housekeeping called '5s system'. There are 5 Japanese words which start with the English letter "S". They don't expect us to do great actions, but very simple and basic actions of sorting out and eliminating unnecessary things, systematic arrangement of things, cleaning the place to have serene atmosphere around us and to have positive attitude to do the above actions consistently. My son, this can be applied not only to material things, but to our minds with little understanding."

Krithik and Kavitha frowned and the question marks were clearly visible on their faces.

"See, how beautiful our house and surrounding is, when we keep them clean and serene!

Our mind is much higher than our house. May be, it can be compared with temple! Do you want to throw any trash inside the temple? Certainly not! So, like 5 "S" system, if we keep the mind clean without loading any dirty information, then the peace is assured. Not only that, the clean mind can only think properly and can recall the memory at appropriate time. You need not search it for long", he concluded.

Both faces of Kavitha and Krithik glowed with the right understanding.

*****

19-17

WHERE THE MIND IS WITHOUT FEAR

"**I** am too scared to travel by plane......"

Kavitha was expressing her fear to her husband. She could feel a lump of pain spiraling from her abdomen when she mentally recalled the scene of plane crash recently shown in the TV.

"There is no other way. The trains are fully booked until end of May." Kavitha's husband replied.

"Ma, please, accept dad's suggestion, ma! If we don't have any trip in this summer holidays, I will have to lose my face in front of my friends" Krithik requested Kavitha. He started to worry over the fear of thinking of his teasing friends.

"Ok! I accept" Kavitha finally gave relief to Krithik's worrying mind.

The fear of her son getting some embarrassment among his friends suppressed her original fear.

The day of their travel arrived.

The fear of leaving the house being closed for about a week just started to haunt the minds of Kavitha.

"See! We are away from our place for one week. What, if some burglary happens? Shall I bring all the jewels with me" She asked her husband.

"See! Already I am having enough of my own fears.. I am thinking what to do in the event of losing my credit card and our tickets and what to do if our expenditure exceeds my credit limit…...so, keep your fears with you", he snorted.

"Ok! Now, tell me, may we be rest assured that you have you already booked the hotel?"

Kavitha came up with new fear!

"No! It is also in the waiting list, Hope we can get it"

"What? Are you joking?. Are we making the trip without the hotel confirmation?! Are we going to stay in the street, if the hotel rooms are not available?" Kavitha was totally out of control with this fear!

Watching those scenes, Krithik started to worry whether the trip would be there or not. Out of that new fear, he started praying the Lord Almighty!

The story goes on like this…….with more added fears.

Do you think the trip will be a pleasant one for the above family even if they managed to fix the trip?

Certainly not!

Still they are yet to encounter some other fears during the journey like whether the weather would be ok or not, or, the foods would be ok or not, or, what if anybody fall sick, etc.

Actually the fears are often out of proportion with actual risk.

How many times the killer SARS had stimulated our adrenal gland when factually the SARS's effect was less when compared to influenza. SARS has killed 774, yet it is scary, since it is unfamiliar. Good old influenza doesn't faze us much, but it kills millions of people every year.

Simply speaking, the fear evolves out of ignorance and lack of confidence, and, mostly from the lessons we got from our parents during our childhood period.

Parents, to get the results they wanted from their children, attempt to narrate fearful events and stories which enter into the subconscious minds of the children. These are really are very difficult to overcome at later on stage.

As the great poet Rabindranath Tagore told us, let us, the responsible parents, help our children live in a country where the minds are without fear!

And the fear should be for unethical things only!

*****

19-18

Sharing the happiness to attain eternal bliss

For Krithik, the bell, mounted in front of the temple, is very high.

He almost raised his body on his toes, but still he could not reach the bell cord. If at all, he managed to catch the cord, he could not give enough swing to the clapper to strike the bell to make sound.

Kavitha could not control her laughs on seeing him struggling to strike the bell.

"Do you want to strike the bell?" she asked.

"Yes, ma, please help me."

She lifted Krithik and assisted him to strike the bell. Krithik rang the bell continuously until Kavitha let him down when her shoulders started to pain her.

"Krithik, why you are so curious to strike the bell?" she asked.

"Ma, when you were worshipping the God, suddenly the bell rang. At that time you told me that it would be a good fortune to hear the sound of the bell when we were praying the Lord. You said our prayers had been accepted by the Lord, Now, see, still many persons are praying, but nobody is here to sound the bell. That is why I would like to strike the bell to make the Lord answer their prayers!"

Kavitha stared at him for a second, then thought, 'It is nothing wrong in saying that the children are Gods! They are not only thinking about themselves, but also would like to share all the good things to the world which they enjoy. We, the adults, are the ones who got adulterated at certain point of time while growing! Where we missed these qualities??"

Kavitha stood still wondering how happy he was. while ringing the bells for others, until Krithik's voice brought her consciousness back.

When we foster the good childhood characters continuously throughout our life, our life would be much cheerful. And we will always be in eternal bliss!

*****

19-19

TUNNEL VISION (TO LEARN FROM THE BIRDS)

The Volkswagen -Polo car was speeding up at eighty km per hour on NH45 road.

"If we are late, we may not be able to watch birds" Kavitha was telling her husband who was driving the car.

"No, I won't raise the speed beyond this limit. Don't worry! The birds will be waiting for us"

While saying this, he suddenly put the gear to third and slowed down the car to avert it from colliding with the bike in front which suddenly slowed down to turn right without a proper signal.

"Ooph! Always safety first! See what happened just now! If we had been fast what would have happened?" he advised Kavitha.

About one hour had elapsed since they started journey from Chennai to Vedanthangal.

By distance, even though the Vedanthangal is 75 Km from Chennai, it took two hours for them to reach Vedanthangal, as sometimes they almost lost in the wrong routes and had to enquire for proper route then and there.

While reaching Vedanthangal it was around 10.30 am. The climate was so wonderful.

After getting the entrance tickets (for them as well as for the camera and the binocular), they entered into a finely created structure which let them into a sidewalk on one side of the lake.

The lake was stretched into about a kilometer and was full of colorful birds. It was a feast to their eyes on seeing the beautiful natural scene and feast to their ears while hearing the chirps from the birds. Some birds reminded of an airplane while they landed and took off from the water-surface.

It was awesome to Krithik to watch more than thousands of colorful birds at one place and funny to watch some birds fighting each other for reserving some seats in the already crowded trees.

"Can you tell the name of the bird, ma?" He asked his mother.

But, the reply came from his father as Kavitha's face showed some sort of "I don't know" signal.

"See there! They are Pelicans! They are Pintails! And these are grey wag tail!"

The father went on telling the names of the birds, but Krithik had to put more efforts to train his mouth to even pronounce them again.

"Father, are these birds are living here throughout the year" Krithik asked.

"No, Krithik! They are migratory birds coming from the countries far away from here, may be, more than 3000 miles apart!"

Krithik's eyes widened with amazement, "Then, why do they migrate and how could they find their ways to this place from their home-place?" He wondered.

"It is still mystery, Krithik! There are so many schools of thought. The reasons are complex and not fully understood. Migration gives birds a huge advantage in finding new sources of food and good places to breed. Studies suggest birds orientate themselves to the compass points using the position of the sun during the day, and the stars at night. They can also sense magnetic north. In addition they use other clues such as visual layout of the land, smell (of the sea), sound (waves on shores, winds through mountain passes).

"The most amazing aspect of bird migration is that the location, route and perhaps even the techniques are hardwired into their brains. Many migrating birds abandon their young as soon as they fledge, and a short time later, the young make the migration on their own."

The father gave Krithik and Kavitha all information about the birds and their migration like an instructor and a tour guide.

"If such good habits are hard-wired into our brains, will it be easier for us to reach our goals and destinations, won't it be, father?"

The sudden question from Krithik made the father speechless for a moment.

At the same time he heard a giggle which came from an old man who had been coming along with them.

All Kavitha's family gave an enquiring look at the old man.

"That can be done, my boy! Through certain yoga and meditation practices we can focus our mind, have a tunnel vision and reach our goals without being diverted by unwanted things," The old man preached like a saint.

At the end of the day Kavitha's family were very happy as they enjoyed the visit to the bird sanctuary and in the mean time they could learn something from the nature.

*****

19-20

LEARNING TO VENT EMOTIONS

As the roller coaster started to decline from the upper most position, Krithik expected lots of screeches and screams to fill the air around THE WONDER LAND, a theme park!.

But, alas!

Except some giggles and some low pitched screams, nothing he could hear!

His mother Kavitha who was sitting nearby him was almost motionless! She seemed like a robot with emotionless face.

She seemed as if frozen with slightly extended lips, meaning she was enjoying the game.

When the roller coaster pulled up and stopped at its home position, Krithik asked Kavitha, "Ma, did you enjoy the ride?"

"Yes, of course, Krithik" she replied.

"It seemed as if you were frightened, didn't you, ma?"

Kavitha gave a little smile as an answer.

"Ok, Ma, Shall we have a lunch? I am hungry."

"Oh sure! Which cuisine do you like?"

"May we try Chinese, Ma?"

At the Chinese restaurant, Krithik was enjoying the delicious chicken variety.

"Oh! What a delicious one!" He expressed his enjoyment with little high voice.

"Usshhh!" Keeping her right index finger on her mouth Kavitha asked him to be silent.

"Why ma?" Krithik asked.

"We should not make such noises in the public, just enjoy yourself" was the answer from Kavitha.

With a murmur, Krithik continued to eat silently.

If we extend this story, still you can find many incidences in which the children would be asked or taught to retain the emotions within themselves.

In due course, children raised in this environment would understand that showing our emotions would be an inhuman thing.

I have seen an employer who always wanted his employees to think he is very strong in nature.

He was a very good entrepreneur who managed his business by maintaining his emotional composure no matter what was happening around him.

If an employee sued him for some ridiculous reason, he never expressed how angry he really felt about the lawsuit. When his competitor under priced him on a major client, he just acted unaffected. If he got mad at a staff member he would just boil inside without venting any of these negative emotions.

Unfortunately, he became the victim to heart attack!

Clearly, swallowed feelings can manifest in very negative ways. It is critical to learn how to appropriately vent our emotions. In order to do so, you first must recognize that you have them.

It is so easy for people to go numb and avoid their feelings, but when they are ignored, feelings just continue to build up. Learning to feel joy, sadness, anger, fear, guilt and pride will allow you to do something about them.

Hence, let us understand that until there is no harm to others there is nothing wrong in expressing our feelings and emotions. This will make us a real living human.

And, let us make our children (who may not be 100 % population of today, but 100% of future) to learn to vent the emotions, by simply not preventing them while they let off emotions.

*****

19-21

MYSTERY OF MIND!

It was around 7:30 pm. The rain was lashing the ground!

The noise of the shower along with the sound of thunder made the darkness outside little more horrifying!

Krithik and his father were waiting at the dining table.

Krithik gave a shout requesting his mother Kavitha. "Ma, please add little more ghee on the dosa"

"How long should I wait if all the dosas you make are going to Krithik?" Krithik's father grunted.

"Don't worry! I am making dosa for both of you simultaneously as I use two pans. Now I am bringing............"

Before she finished her words, the darkness suddenly surrounded them all.

The next moment Krithik and his father could hear some noise as if somebody was falling down and then they felt something, probably the pieces of dosa hitting on their faces.

"Oh! I slipped! The poor power outage!" With many curses Kavitha stood on her foot slowly collecting the plate and other pieces of Dosa after her husband lighted on his mobile phone.

"Why were you so hurrying?" the husband started to advise her," Just it took only 30 seconds for me to reach my mobile phone and switch on its light!"

Kavitha did not tell why she suddenly did run from the kitchen immediately after the power failure. She thought she might be teased by them if she revealed the reason.

she actually got frightened on seeing the darkness through the window and saw some illusions in her mind that had been haunting her since she saw the horror movie- "Kanjana".

Instead of telling the real truth, she mumbled, "The person who took the UPS for repairing is so lethargic that even after two days he is not bringing it repaired!"

"Why there were no power cuts last week?"

Krithik innocently asked his parents hoping to get reply from any one of them.

"There was an election last week"- came the reply in chorus from his parents!

"What the correlation?" Krithik enquired them.

"If there were frequent power cuts during election, chances are there that people will get irritated and they would vote against the ruling party" the father explained.

"How come they would forget those power cuts which they suffered one week before? And, how come the politician could think for sure that the people would vote for them if they could maintain uninterrupted power just for a week before election?"

Krithik asked the right question.

"That is the nature of human. The Lord has given us the boon to forget the past as the time passes on and remember only the recent happenings. Neglecting this boon, if we continue to dwell on our past delving the reasons for why it happened, then happiness do not have any room to dwell inside us. However, the boon has negative side also! The boss would take biased decisions during appraisal of his subordinate if he emotionally considers only the recent deeds done by the subordinate. " while replying, the father's mind drifted towards his office affairs.

"But…., why the horror scenes that we have seen are not getting away from our mind so quickly?" Now, Kavitha's question brought the father's mind back.

"It depends upon how repeatedly you allow your mind to replay the scenes. Practice to feed good new things to our mind continuously"

While he was replying, the power came back. A clear vision came back to their eyes through the lights and to their minds through the discussion.

They were very happy in unraveling the mystery of mind to some extent.

*****

19-22

Gratitude- the animal style

No sooner, the dog heard the voice of Krithik, it almost pranced on him, rapidly wagging its tail.

The dog started to lick his legs.

Krithik looked into the eyes of the dog as if he was searching something. The eyes showed nothing other than the kindness and love.

Krithik ran his fingers through the furs behind the neck of the dog and patted gently on its back.

"I am so sorry, dear," Krithik whispered into the ears of the dog.

With this gentle treatment from Krithik, the dog slightly barked to express its happiness.

Then, Krithik gave some biscuits to it. When the dog was eating the biscuits happily, he started to recall the incidence happened in the morning.

He was in hurry to school in the morning. As he had slept a little bit longer than usual, all the subsequent timings of his routine schedule got disturbed.

The trouble started when he was about to leave the house.

The dog!

It, biting his school bag, did not allow him to leave. Its actions conveyed the meaning that it wanted to play with Krithik.

"Is it the right time to play? I am in hurry! Please let me go!" Krithik told the dog.

However, its persistent pulling of his bag made Krithik mad.

Out of fury, he kicked off the dog with his legs. The dog flew in the air for some time before it hit the ground.

Might have been a heavy blow!

The dog let out a mournful howl.

However, it did not attempt to bite back, nor attack Krithik. Instead, it toiled away from the house.

Now, on seeing the expression of gratitude by the dog, Krithik's eyes started to water, "Oh! What a lesson on gratitude that I am learning from my dog! If everybody develops and has this kind of attitude towards gratitude, the peace is assured and the love will be prevailing everywhere!"

Krithik decided not to be the cause for a bad incidence again.

If we want to understand how to live higher quality lives with each other and other creatures on this planet, we have to look no further than our furry, flying, flowing, and feathered friends. Animals offer us some of the most enduring and endearing examples of spiritual values.

The spiritual quality of gratitude is one important quality that soothes the grinding of daily life.

When you are out in nature or relaxing at home, sit quietly, close your eyes, and reflect on the question: What is love? Fill yourself with gratitude for the blessings that are all around you. Be alert to the subtle yet profound ways your question may be answered.

Gratitude- A spiritual virtue that leads to respect for life and for all creatures!

We can learn it from the animals.

*****

19-23

LET THE FRUIT TO RIPE NATURALLY

"**M**a! Please enroll my name in the key board class, ma!"

"Ma! I wish to join music class"

"Ma...Karate class! Please ma!'

"Ma! See, how neatly I have drawn the picture of poke-man! May I join in the drawing class also?"

These were the requests (most correctly" tortures") from Krithik two years before.

Krithik had been enrolled into whatever the new class available at that time to learn new talents.

Every day, after returning from those classes, Krithik used to show his expertise to his parents and impress them about his ability to learn new things quickly. In the evening hours after schooling and during holidays he would immerse himself and enjoy himself in practicing whatever he had learnt.

Now?

Two years have elapsed.

The scene has changed.

He is seemed as if he has been drained off of all his enthusiasm!

Leave alone showing of his dexterity and talents to others, now a days he is not at all showing any interest even going to these classes!

Kavitha had been in pride of his son's talents especially when boasting herself in front of her friends, but, now, she could not believe herself about the changes in the attitude of her son.

She had been expecting her son to be the number one personality in all areas! However, his recent attitude of not showing any interest even in his regular studies worried her.

Finally she decided to ask her son.

"Krithik! What happened to you? Why don't you show any interest to go to music and key board classes? And even to your school? Your grade is steeply declining! After all you only wished and selected these classes two years before! Tell me. Don't you want to become a great man?"

Krithik, who had been bowing his head so far, slowly lifted his head and shot back her, "Ma! This is,,,,this is the one which made me to lose all my interest!. Everybody, including you, expects me to do the best in the world! Actually I wanted to learn new things for me to enjoy and not to impress anybody nor to become a great man in that field!...."

Kavitha never expected such a feedback from his son.

Even though she got angry at first slowly she came to realize her mistakes. She recalled how she had been forcing him and insisting him to get good grade in all subjects and not encouraging him to enjoy the learning.

Such kind of activities of parents and responses from children can be called by any name in psychology!

But, it is natural truth that the job of parents is limited just to support their siblings to learn naturally and not to force them.

We cannot get the fruits riped by simply beating. We have to provide the best suitable environment for the fruits to ripe naturally!

*****

19-24

NEIGHBOURS' ENVY

Kavitha and Krithik could not believe their eyes!

They could see as if every character from the movie is coming out of the TV. Sometimes, they had to dodge themselves to avoid the illusory stones being thrown out of TV screen. The birds and beautiful butterflies were seemed flying very nearer to them.

They were watching 3-D Sony Television in their neighbor's house!

When they were invited by the neighbor, Kavitha showed some reluctance initially as she sensed little pride in the eyes of her neighbor which created some sort of jealousy in her.

"The price is about Rs 150,000! Actually we got it free through lucky draw when we booked our new BMW car!"

As the neighbor continued to flatter, Kavitha could not control the temperature being raised out of envy inside her body.

Appreciating her luck she returned to her house along with Krithik.

Now, about ten days had elapsed since they had 3-D experience.

Kavitha was almost fuming at all things. She almost stopped talking with her neighbor. She could not lead normal life as the negative ego and jealousy took the control of her mind.

On the eleventh day morning when she was busy in the kitchen and still thinking about the lucky abundance what the neighbor has got, she overheard Krithik's voice from the living room.

"Ma! Come and see here! Very interesting news in the news paper!"

"No! I am in the kitchen! I will see it afterwards" -her reply and the tone clearly revealed her unwillingness.

Krithik directly came into the kitchen.

"Ma! See How big and beautiful the house is!. This house is built by Mr. Mukesh Ambani- the Chairman of Reliance! The cost is Rs 2000 crore!"

Still, Kavitha did not show any interest!

"Ma! Why don't you be jealous of Mukesh Ambani? I could understand your jealousness with our neighbor when she bought BMW car and 3D TV. But, I can't understand why don't you extend the same thing towards Ambani's fortune?"

Kavitha turned and looked deeply her son. "He has grown up. He is asking this question with an intention", she thought.

He, however, continued to tell her with a sort of worry in his tone. "For the past ten days your envy with our neighbor almost has deprived us of all our happiness!"

It seemed to Kavitha as if she was beaten up by some imaginary hands from nowhere!

The negative ego with her neighbor vanished suddenly.

Now a smile came to play on her lips. "You are right, Krithik. I have made a mistake. When comes to jealousness, why we envy our neighbor rather than unknown fortunate person?

If getting envy is my natural character, then why don't I envy Ambani? The sarcastic envy is so clever that it only play with close persons and will not get rest until they are being separated. Why should we give such a chance to this kind of Satan? Hereafter I will not give any place for him in my mind."

With that the happiness re entered the house.

*****

19-25

NO SHORT CUT FOR THE SUCCESS

The melodious voice of that singer was so beautiful that it almost held every audience like a spell.

The nodding of heads and hands out of fascination in tune with the rhythm seemed like the wave patterns formed by a smooth and gentle flow of air on grasses in the field.

It was carnatic musical concert. The singer provided a great rendition through accurate and appropriate Arohanas and Avarohanas.

He did not misplace any swaram (note) in all sort of Raagas. When he explained and then demonstrated on how the melakarta raagas like Kalyani. Hanumatodi,

Natabairavi, Kharaharapriya and Harikambhoji were yielded on applying Graha Bedam (shifting of tonic note) on Shankarabharanam, the audience applauded loudly.

"Ma! How is it possible for him to sing like this?" Krithik asked his mother Kavitha.

"He is lucky, my boy! Lucky to have such voice and talent" she replied her son.

"Why don't we have such talents? Are we unlucky?" Krithik's voice showed some worry.

However, his question went off into the air unanswered.

Even though, he enjoyed the music, when he came out of the hall, he felt some unexplainable heaviness in his chest.

That incidence and the feeling slowly faded away in the coming days as he immersed himself in the daily chores of school activities.

However, the same sort of hurt feeling crept into his mind again when he and his mother were watching an English movie in TV. The hero in that movie was so strong and with lot of muscles he bombarded the enemies so easily!

"The hero is so lucky to have such strong body, isn't it, ma?" Krithik asked with a great sigh.

Kavitha noticed some sort of loss of confidence in her son's voice. So, she simply nodded her head instead of answering.

Some days passed!

Krithik was showing his progress-report card to his mother.

It was a great shock to Kavitha.

She could not believe her own eyes.

His progress was on negative side, with minimum marks in English paper.

"WHY?....." She attempted to shout, but something seemed stuck in her throat.

"Ma! What shall I do ma? I am not so lucky to be born with such learning power..........."

Krithik tried to justify his inefficiency.

Kavitha stood speechless for hours.

This is a typical incidence which shows our lack of awareness in showing right path to our children for the success.

Remember, there is no short cut for the success! We don't know how much effort that the singer in this story might have put in before he appeared in front of the audience.

In the book OUTLIERS, Mr Malcom Gladwel writes that those (like Bill gates and Steve Jobs) who became the best in their field put in no less than 10000 hours of work to master their skill. We need to put in time to be the best we can, in that area. Whether we have to work overtime and forgo hanging out, that's what it takes. That's what it has cost every one we admire. If we want their success, we also have to put in their sacrifice. To live like nobody lives, we have to work like nobody works.

Let us make our children to understand that there is no short cut for the success, like LUCK, other than persistent and consistent working.

*****

19-26

WASTING FOOD? YOU ARE FINED!

"**Y**ou are punished! Pay Rs 50 as a fine for this kind of act!"

Krithik startled when he heard that sharp and rasping voice.

Before he could recover, he could see a bill for Rs 50 being produced in front of his face by a steel hand.

Controlling his emotions, he attempted to identify the person standing in front of him.

"The person… it is not a person! it is….. a robot?!!!" A mixed feeling ran into Krithik's mind.

Summoning his courage he asked the robot, "who are you to punish me?"

"I am a robot! My mission is to protect the earth from food wastages. I found you wasting two idlis by throwing away into the dust bin. That is why you are punished! Now you pay the amount by depositing in to the account number written on the bill on any nationalized bank."
Saying this, the robot went away swiftly with a whiz.

"I could smell some other idiot is wasting the food……." Krithik could hear progressively diminishing voice of that robot as it disappeared from his eyes.

To his surprise the same robot reappeared again in the morning in front of him and his mother Kavitha when she was packing his Tiffin box with food.

Kavitha screeched by the sudden sight of the robot.

"Madam! You better know that your son will not eat that much amount of food in the afternoon. What he will do if he finds it excess? Simply throw away as waste! So, being the root cause for such waste you are fined Rs 50! Have the bill. The payment details are overleaf!"

The robot quickly tucked the bill into her palms and soon vanished.

Kavitha stood like a statue for some moments.

Some months later.

The leader of the state was addressing in the TV channel.

"My fellow citizens! I am very happy to announce that through our new mission 'prevent food waste'; we could increase the availability of food as much as 40% of its production. I sincerely thank you for your kind co-operation to make our mission a great success!......"

The leader's voice slowly faded away when Kavitha's voice took over its place.

"Krithik! Wake up! You will be late if you sleep like this" Kavitha's voice roused him out of the bed.

"Hmm! After all it was a dream!" he murmured himself with a smile.

If Krithik's dream becomes true, our world can save enormous amount of food.

Psychology can be useful in helping reduce food waste. There are two ways we can reduce food waste, either prevent consumers from throwing away huge amounts of food as waste, or stop them in some way from producing so much.

Once people begin a certain behavior in their lives, it is difficult to discourage it. So rather than discouraging them from wasting food, it is easier for someone to act as a good influence on them not to even begin wasting food in the first place.

As children, it is easier to establish a social norm for them, but it is harder for them to change it later in their lives. We can establish a form of positive punishment to the child.

*****

19-27

WHO STOLE MY JUICE?

"**M**a, who stole my juice?"

Krithik came to Kavitha complaining with a sad face.

"What happened?" She asked him.

"Yesterday I had kept one glassful of juice inside the fridge. Now, some portion is missing…"

"Don't worry Krithik! Some portion would have evaporated. Nobody would dare to take your juice"

He was confused "where does all the evaporation go, ma!?"

"To the atmosphere…!"

Krithik seemed not to give up in asking further questions.

"Why should it evaporate?"

"It is natural law to make everything equilibrium" Kavitha replied him calmly.

"Please ma, explain about equilibrium"

"The air surrounding us could hold certain amount of water vapour. If it has some deficiency it would receive the water in the form of vapor from the place where it is plenty. In your case, from the juice!"

Kavitha, now, was seemed satisfied herself as if she had fully explained.

But, after some thoughtful moments there came a question from Krithik again!

"Is it applicable to all the things, ma!? Tell me, is it ok for someone who doesn't have enough money to take it from the other who is rich with abundant money?"

Kavitha, eventhough did not expect such type of question from Krithik, tried to answer him.

"No, Krithik, No!,. Here the thing you have to notice is that in the nature, the 'haves' would give to' have nots'. The Plenty automatically flows to deficient places to make everything equilibrium. So, the answer for your question is that the poor person should not take himself the money from the rich, the act of which would otherwise be called as theft".

Krithik was now almost convinced and drew the conclusion, "Now, I understand. Actually the "rich" has to give. If we follow the nature in giving whatever excess we have, whether it is knowledge or love or money, won't our world be in prosperous and peaceful, Ma?"

As Krithik was quickly catching up her point, she was happy.

"But, for that there is a limit. By giving and sharing one should not make the other lazy. Keeping this in our mind if we follow the natural law, certainly there will be a universal peace!"

Kavitha concluded.

*****